Marshall W. Meyer

Bureaucratic Structure and Authority

COORDINATION
AND CONTROL
IN 254 GOVERNMENT
AGENCIES

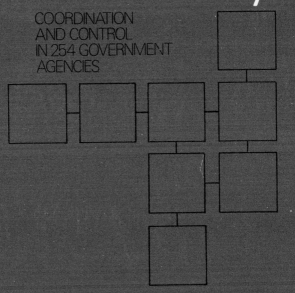

Bureaucratic Structure and Authority

Marshall W. Meyer
Cornell University

Bureaucratic Structure and Authority

COORDINATION
AND CONTROL
IN 254 GOVERNMENT
AGENCIES

Harper & Row, Publishers
New York/Evanston/San Francisco/London

For Judith,
with love

Bureaucratic Structure and Authority:
Coordination and Control in 254 Government Agencies

Copyright © 1972 by Marshall W. Meyer

Standard Book Number: 06-044426-6

Library of Congress Catalog Card Number: 72-76372

Contents

Preface

This book, though based on quantitative data, is a conceptual inquiry into how organizations function. It assumes that organizations, like all social systems, seek to elicit more or less ordered behavior from their members through the use of authority, or, to use Weber's phrase, imperative coordination. It also assumes that authority is ubiquitous in organizations but may take different forms—some so obvious as to be repugnant, others so subtle that they all but escape notice. Authority may be exercised through commands, rules and regulations, or professional groups whose members adhere to standards that may be in conflict with expectations of bureaucratic superiors. A further assumption is that formal structures of organizations vary and that these variations can be meaningfully related to patterns of authority. This book, then, will attempt to link structural attributes of bureaucracies to the authority exercised within them.

Sociological theory tells us that authority is a property of social systems, not of individual people. This book attempts to take that assertion seriously by dealing with organizations as wholes and relating patterns of coordination to other attributes. It should be read as an exploratory study, as suggestive of hypotheses if not conclusive in its findings.

One concern of contemporary organization theory has been the impact of environment and technology on the behavior of organizations and the people who happen to be in them. This concern is not overlooked here, but it is downplayed. The government agencies which are the focus of this book are much less affected by environmental contingencies and technological change than other types of organizations. They were chosen for this study, in part, because of their stability, as the intention was to assess the mutual interrelations of *organizational* characteristics. These interrelations have appeared sometimes in complex and contradictory patterns which suggest that simple causal models may be inadequate to describe organizational processes. To assert that equilibrium pervades organizations does not foreclose the possibility of empirical research. Quite the contrary, it calls for data describing organizations at different points in time—longitudinal data—which allow propositions involving two-way causation to be tested directly rather than by inference. Such data are now being gathered on the 254 government bureaus described in this volume.

Sooner or later we will have to have precise knowledge of how complex social systems work, if only for purposes of planning. If the conclusions of this book in any way anticipate what will be learned, the social scientific enterprise is likely to be frustrating. The reader will note a recurring pattern in this study: Changes in organizations give rise to opposing forces which tend to nullify one another. Structural changes conducive to decentralization of decision, for instance, are accompanied by rules and regulations which largely determine decisions in advance. Change leads to no change; an equilibrium of sorts is maintained. The structural-functionalists have been saying this for years, but hardly anyone has bothered to listen, perhaps because it is not considered "relevant." May I suggest that nothing could be more relevant to those who are seriously dedicated to social change?

This study of 254 city, county, and state departments of finance was one of the projects of the Comparative Organization Research Program at the University of Chicago.[1] CORP was supported by National Science Foundation Grant GS-553, which is gratefully acknowledged. The Harvard University Program on Technology and Society financed some additional analysis of the data and the excursion into industry described in Chapter 6. Special thanks are due the Municipal Finance Officers Association of the United States

---

[1] This book is report number 16 of the Comparative Organization Research Program.

and Canada for their endorsement of this research. Robert Funk, MFOA's Director of Research, was especially helpful. The Field Department of the National Opinion Research Center is commended for completing 97 percent of the assigned interviews through the efforts of Mrs. Eve Weinberg and her staff.

A number of people have read and commented upon this manuscript. Howard Aldrich, Richard Hall, and William Foote Whyte were the most critical and therefore the most helpful reviewers. They are hereby absolved of responsibility for any flaws that escaped their scrutiny. However, my wife Judith is not. It was her intention to make this a perfect book.

An intellectual and personal debt to Professor Peter M. Blau must be acknowledged here. As director of the Comparative Organization Research Program, he supervised the design of the study and collection of the data in 1966. Blau then went to Cambridge as Pitt Professor of American History and Institutions for the 1966-1967 academic year, leaving me to pursue a line of inquiry that, as it turns out, was quite different from his own. Blau and I have disagreed, privately and in print, on the analysis of data on organizations.[2] His is a rigorous approach that insists that the data strongly confirm propositions, while mine is more intuitive and places less emphasis on confirmation than on the substance of ideas themselves. Despite our differences or because of them, Blau has been the most helpful and supportive critic of my work, and his influence is reflected throughout this book.

Portions of Chapter 3 appear in the September 1968 issue of *Administrative Science Quarterly*. Chapter 4 was originally published in somewhat different form in the *American Journal of Sociology*, November 1968.

M. W. M.

---

[2] See, for instance, Marshall W. Meyer, "Some Constraints in Analyzing Data on Organizational Structures," *American Sociological Review*, 36 (1971), 294-97, and Blau's comments, *Ibid*., 304-307.

1
Rationality and Authority in Bureaucratic Administration

We begin with a familiar idea: Organizational rationality, because it operates through authority relationships and super- and subordination, threatens human rationality. We suggest that this need not be the case, that in fact bureaucratic organizations can minimize overt authority and subordination. The study of organizational structures is introduced as a means of testing this idea, and the concept of authority is discussed and extended so that it applies to more than relationships between formally designated supervisors and subordinates. The design of the empirical study and the plan of the book are reviewed at the end of the chapter.

CRITIQUES OF BUREAUCRACY

Perhaps more than any other form of social organization, bureaucracy embodies the values of rationality and impersonality that have come to dominate modern societies. As Weber put it, "Precision, speed, unambiguity, knowledge of the files, continuity, discretion, unity, strict subordination, reduction of friction and of material and personal costs—these are raised to the optimum point in the strictly bureaucratic administration." He continues, "Its specific nature . . . develops the more perfectly the more bureaucracy is 'dehumanized,' the more completely it succeeds in eliminating from official business love, hatred, and all purely personal, irrational, and emotional elements which escape

1

calculation."[1] Few social scientists have questioned the values of rationality and impersonality. Indeed, contemporary theories of change argue that social structures become increasingly rationalized as processes of differentiation and the emergence of universalistic values continue.[2] Although no one will argue against rationality as such, many critics are fearful of rational organization and its consequences. Bureaucracy is suspect. Some critics contend that bureaucracy is so rational and so efficient that it dominates and controls rather than serves its members and clients. Others, ironically, attack bureaucracy for its supposed inefficiency. Lacking the profit motive, it is argued, government bureaus must operate according to inflexible rules and regulations which are both cumbersome and insensitive to special needs of clients.

There have been a number of other critiques of bureaucratic organization. One is that bureaucracy is incompatible with democratic values. Michels, in his study *Political Parties,* and many others have made this argument.[3] Concentration of the means of administration in the hands of a few experts makes the leadership indispensable and insensitive to the needs of members, they contend. Another critique is that bureaucracy subverts organizational goals. Much of the literature on bureaucratic dysfunctions, especially Merton's "Bureaucratic Structure and Personality," stresses this point. Displacement of goals—the substitution of organizational means for organizational ends—results from bureaucracy's need to elicit predictable behavior from its members through binding rules and regulations.[4] This critique of bureaucracy, then, posits necessary conflict between goals that disrupt bureaucratic routine and the self-maintenance needs of organizations. Bureaucracy limits the kinds of goals an organization can pursue, and it restricts the extent to which organizations can adapt to new situations.

Underlying these views of bureaucracy is a pervasive question: Is the rationality of bureaucratic organization to be identified with what is

---

[1] Max Weber, "Bureaucracy," in *From Max Weber: Essays in Sociology,* eds. H. Gerth and C. W. Mills (New York: Oxford University Press, 1958), p. 214.
[2] See, for example, Talcott Parsons, *The Social System* (New York: Free Press, 1951), pp. 195-206.
[3] Robert Michels, *Political Parties,* trans. E. Paul and C. Paul (New York: Free Press, 1949). See also Gaetano Mosca, *The Ruling Class* (New York: McGraw-Hill, 1939).
[4] Robert K. Merton, "Bureaucratic Structure and Personality," in *Social Theory and Social Structure,* 2d ed. rev. (New York: Free Press, 1957), pp. 195-206.

rational for individual persons? For the most part, the critics have answered no. Karl Mannheim, for example, has devised the concepts of *functional rationality* and *substantial rationality* to show how bureaucracy develops its own logic that bears little relationship to what is rational for individual persons. Functional rationality, according to Mannheim, is "a series of actions . . . organized in such a way that it leads to a previously defined goal, every element in this series of actions receiving a functional position and role."[5] The important point is that one can act in a functionally rational manner toward irrational ends, for example, methodically exterminating a race of people. Functional rationality does not question ends; it only demands that one use the most efficient means to attain the ends which others have specified. Substantial rationality, by contrast, is the "capacity to act intelligently in a given situation on the basis of one's own insight into the interrelations of events."[6] A person uses his intellect to reason appropriate goals and means to these goals, and he questions the goals that others may impose upon him. Though Mannheim perceives the difference between functional and substantial rationality as absolute, it is in fact a relative one. Functional rationality requires that one search only for means to a goal, whereas substantial rationality involves elaboration of new goals. New goals and new values, however, are usually derived from more general cultural prescriptions, and in this sense the same kind of means-ends relationship that characterizes functional rationality is also true of substantial rationality. The difference between the two is that substantial rationality demands much more thought and reflection than does functional rationality. In short, functionally rational behavior allows only limited discretion to a person, while substantial rationality demands much more judgment.

Mannheim contends that modern industrial society increasingly substitutes functional for substantial rationality. As society becomes organized to accomplish objective ends, the capacity to determine goals is reserved to fewer and fewer people. Most people, then, become unable or unwilling to maintain their individuality and their ability to understand situations. "Functional rationalization, is, in its very nature, bound to deprive the average individual of thought, insight, and

[5]Karl Mannheim, *Man and Society in an Age of Reconstruction* (New York: Harcourt Brace Jovanovich, 1941), p. 53.
[6]*Ibid.*, p. 58.

responsibility, and to transfer these capacities to individuals who direct the process of rationalization."[7] Thus, in Mannheim's view, bureaucratic organization as the agent of functional rationalization is rational only for the planners, the managers.

Though much of Mannheim's concern about the decline of individual autonomy can be attributed to his experience in pre-World War II Nazi Germany, some of what he argues is also drawn from Max Weber's ideas about bureaucratic organization. Two attributes of Weber's model of bureaucracy, in addition to the stands of efficiency and impersonality cited above, would seem to contribute to functional rationality. First, according to Weber, bureaucracy is characterized by a high degree of division of labor and specialization of employees. An employee's jurisdiction, his authority to give commands and make decisions, is strictly limited. If a member of a bureaucracy is faced with a problem he lacks the authority to resolve, then he must refer it to a superior. Intensive division of labor, in conjunction with regulations that constrain an official's discretion in handling his tasks, very much limits the extent to which a bureaucrat can act intelligently on the basis of his insight. Second, bureaucratic organization in Weber's model includes a hierarchical ordering of positions such that there are "higher" and "lower" offices, with the lower positions reporting to the higher ones. Implicit is the notion that bureaucracy entails an extremely rigid administrative structure in which all communication must "go through channels." The line of authority is always preserved so that each person can be held accountable for duties assigned to him. But there is another element of hierarchy that may be more important insofar as Mannheim's ideas are concerned. Upper levels of a hierarchy set in advance goals which are to be pursued by subordinate members. As March and Simon observe, each level of hierarchy takes the goals set for it by a higher level and translates them into specific objectives for subordinates to pursue.[8] Nonsupervisory employees, of course, do not participate in this process. A hierarchical authority structure, then, contributes to functional rationality in establishing a system where one person (or level of hierarchy) sets objectives for another. The net result is that the head of the organization, the apex of the hierarchical pyramid, has

[7]Ibid.
[8]James G. March and Herbert A. Simon, *Organizations* (New York: Wiley, 1958), pp. 150-158.

complete discretion in setting goals. His behavior may be substantially rational, but other members of a bureaucracy are limited to actions that contribute to previously defined objectives. The hierarchical structure of bureaucracies as well as intensive division of labor thus contributes to functional rationality.

Weber's model of bureaucracy is an ideal-typical construct, a "one-sided *accentuation* of one or more points of view . . . by the synthesis of many diffuse, discrete, more or less present and occasionally absent *concrete individual* phenomena."[9] As such, it is no hypothesis, and it is not subject to empirical test, at least not directly. We shall continually comment on Weber's notions of bureaucracy, but there will be no attempt to prove or disprove them. Weber's ideal-typical constructs were developed out of a broad knowledge of different types of social structures, and if his model of bureaucracy involves any propositions at all, it posits the uniqueness of the bureaucratic form compared with other types of social organization.[10] Mannheim's observations, however, do involve some propositions that can be confirmed or disconfirmed. Specifically, Mannheim argues that an inevitable result of bureaucratization is centralization of control, whether in whole societies or large-scale organizations. As functional rationality replaces substantial rationality, discretion to make the most important decisions is increasingly reserved to members of a managerial elite. Pluralism in a society or multiple sources of control in large organizations become less likely as bureaucratization proceeds. Ultimately, in Mannheim's view, bureaucratization leads to a form of mass society in which all members are controlled by a ruling clique of planners.

> This is the state of affairs which has led to the growing distance between the elite and the masses, and to the "appeal of the leader" which has recently become so widespread. The average person surrenders part of his own cultural individuality with every new act of integration into a functionally rationalized complex of activities. He becomes increasingly accustomed to being led by others and gradually gives up his own interpretation of events for those which

[9]Max Weber, *The Methodology of the Social Sciences,* trans. E. Shils and H. Finch (New York: Free Press, 1949), p. 90.
[10]A functional interpretation of Weber *derives* other hypotheses from the theory of bureaucracy, but these hypotheses are not stated by Weber. For a functional interpretation of Weber, see Peter M. Blau and W. Richard Scott, *Formal Organizations* (San Francisco: Chandler, 1962), pp. 34-35.

others give him. When the rationalized mechanism of social life collapses in times of crisis, the individual cannot repair it by his own insight.[11]

The only question that then remains, according to Mannheim, is that of "Who plans the planners?"[12]

Methodological Considerations

This study will deal with much the same question that concerned Mannheim, though in a very different manner. Quantitative statistical analysis will be used in place of a discursive approach. We shall inquire if bureaucratic means of administration necessarily remove substantial rationality and concentrate the ability to make meaningful decisions in the hands of a few managers and officials, or if instead organizations can be designed to encourage discretion and wide participation in decisions while at the same time maintaining coordination. In answering this question which applies specifically to large-scale organizations, we hope to gain some understanding of whether or not rational forms of organization in general contribute to the decline of substantial rationality and the consequent centralization of control in society. We hypothesize that bureaucracy does not necessarily remove substantial rationality from people, and that, in fact, forms of rational organization may emerge which protect their members' ability to use their intelligence and judgment as new situations arise. But we also hypothesize that authority (imperative coordination) remains ubiquitous in organizations. In other words, rationality in organizations can contribute to either centralized or more relaxed control, the choice between the two depending partly on the intentions of managers and the capacities of workers, but more importantly on the nature of an organization's tasks and the formal organizational arrangements devised to secure coordination and control.

As stated above, the hypothesis is hardly in a form that allows it to be tested empirically. Two methodological points arise that must be considered before an answer to the broad question posed above can be attempted. The first problem is defining the range of concepts to be used in analyzing bureaucratic organizations. The second problem, one

[11]Mannheim, *Man and Society*, p. 59.
[12]*Ibid.*, p. 75.

closely related to the first, is the choice of a unit of analysis: *What should be studied in order to understand bureaucratic structures?* Answers to these questions are largely arbitrary. Organizations can be studied by examining interpersonal behavior that occurs in bureaucratic settings, by examining structural attributes of bureaucracy, or by examining characteristics of whole societies that affect bureaucratic structures. Human relations theory and sociological studies of so-called "informal" organizations tend to concentrate on the first approach while, by contrast, Weber's theory of bureaucracy and a number of crosscultural studies of organizations take the latter approach.[13]

Perhaps some examples will illustrate the differences between the human relations and the macrosocial perspectives on organizations. In *Management and the Worker,* perhaps the prototype of human relations studies, the authors note why foremen are so frequently criticized by lower supervisors. They observe:

> As a visible representative of authority, the foreman is deprived of that prestige which comes from distance. Yet, more than any other supervisor, he is responsible for maintaining discipline in his department and for upholding the rules of the technical organization by means of which efficiency is maintained. More than any other of his subordinate supervisors, he has to think in terms of cost, efficiency, and output. In spite of his best intentions, he is always in the position of violating the feelings of personal integrity of his subordinates.[14]

In other words, the foreman's role, the constellation of interpersonal relationships and contradictory demands into which he is thrust, accounts for his difficult relations with subordinates.

[13]For some examples of the human relations approach to organizations, see Robert L. Kahn and Daniel Katz, "Leadership Practices in Relation to Productivity and Morale," in *Group Dynamics,* ed. D. Cartwright and A. Zander (New York: Harper & Row, 1962), pp. 554-570. The term "informal organization" was coined by Chester Barnard. See *The Functions of the Executive* (Cambridge, Mass.: Harvard University Press, 1938), p. 115. Some sociological studies of informal organization include Alvin W. Gouldner, *Patterns of Industrial Bureaucracy* (New York: Free Press, 1954), and Peter M. Blau, *The Dynamics of Bureaucracy,* 2d ed. rev. (Chicago: University of Chicago Press, 1963). For some crosscultural comparisons, see James C. Abegglen, *The Japanese Factory* (New York: Free Press, 1958) and Morroe Berger, *Bureaucracy and Society in Modern Egypt* (Princeton, N.J.: Princeton University Press, 1957).

[14]Fritz J. Roethlisberger and William J. Dickson, *Management and the Worker* (Cambridge, Mass.: Harvard University Press, 1939), p. 368.

The macrosocial approach to organizations offers a completely different explanatory paradigm. In discussing why face-to-face authority relationships are so difficult in a French bureaucracy, Crozier notes:

> The prevailing view of authority is still that of universalism and absolutism; it continues to retain something of the seventeenth century's political theory, with its mixture of rationality and *bon plaisir*. The two attitudes are contradictory. However, they can be reconciled within a bureaucratic system, since impersonal rules and centralization make it possible to reconcile an absolutist conception of authority and the elimination of most direct dependence relationships. In other words, the French bureaucratic system of organization is the perfect solution to the basic dilemma of Frenchmen about authority. They cannot bear the omnipotent authority which they feel is indispensable if any kind of cooperative activity is to succeed.[15]

The dilemmas of authority, then, have their origins in French cultural patterns and political traditions; problems of role conflicts and personality differences are not mentioned.

These two approaches to the study of organizations involve very different assumptions. Studies of informal organization and human relations assume implicitly that the formal structure of most organizations is essentially similar. For instance, when it is found that there is an inverse correlation between how closely a foreman supervises his employees and the productivity of his section, it is assumed that this relationship holds regardless of other organizational properties, such as the character of organizational rules or the span of control of supervisors.[16] On the other hand, the macrosocial perspective on bureaucracy assumes, again implicitly, that bureaucratic structure is variable, and that it can be explained for the most part in terms of characteristics of whole societies. It also assumes implicitly that informal patterns and personality differences exert no distinctive influence, except possibly as intervening variables. Weber, for example, writes that bureaucratic administration appears only in the presence of a money economy and the assurance of a steady income for an organization.[17]

---

[15]Michel Crozier, *The Bureaucratic Phenomenon* (Chicago: University of Chicago Press, 1964), p. 222.
[16]Kahn and Katz, "Leadership Practices in Relation to Productivity and Morale," p. 561.
[17]Weber, "Bureaucracy," p. 204.

Crucial Assumptions

Here, organizations will be studied from an approach that is altogether different from the human relations or the macrosocial orientations. The human relations model of organizations is one that is "built-up" from interaction among members; the macrosocial model of bureaucracy posits that organizational forms are derived from general cultural prescriptions and material conditions in a society. (The latter is the "trickle-down" theory.) By contrast to other approaches, organizations will be treated here as more or less closed, self-contained systems. As little attention as possible will be paid to external factors such as cultural and economic variables and personality differences among individual workers. The attempt is to study the internal dynamics of bureaucratic structures: How do changes in certain attributes of organizations have implications for other attributes, particularly the distribution of authority and discretion within an organization?

We do not deny the validity of other approaches which treat organizations as open systems subject to environmental uncertainties and constraints.[18] Indeed, the two perspectives would seem to complement one another. But a deliberate choice is made here to focus on the internal dynamics of organizations. This influenced the selection of organizations included in the present research which are very much of the bureaucratic type, and operate in relatively stable environments.[19] Had we wished to treat bureaucracies as open systems, a very different set of organizations—some faced with uncertainty and external constraint and some not—would have been studied.

The term *bureaucratic structure* needs explanation at this point. Bureaucratic structure includes certain global characteristics of organizations (for example, the use of a computer), relational properties (for example, the fact that eight employees report to a given supervisor), and aggregate properties of complex organizations (for example, the proportion of employees who have a college degree). Bureaucratic structure also includes measures of *organizational* performance

[18]See, for example, James D. Thompson, *Organizations in Action* (New York: McGraw-Hill, 1967) and Shirley Terreberry, "The Evolution of Organizational Environments," *Administrative Science Quarterly*, 12, 1968, 530-613.

[19]Gail S. MacColl's study of 28 administrative units of local governments shows that finance and finance-related departments are subject to much less environmental uncertainty than other government agencies. See "Technology, Environment, and Urban Administration: Problems in Uncertain Design," paper delivered to the American Society of Public Administration, March 1972.

insofar as they can be separated from the behavior of individual members. We assume that most bureaucracies seek to maintain an acceptable level of performance (or effectiveness) without incurring an unacceptable level of unanticipated and undesired consequences (or low efficiency).[20] Where a given attribute of organizational structure impedes effectiveness or efficiency, it is predicted that other organizational attributes will be modified to maintain satisfactory performance. Thus, to anticipate a finding presented later, as the number of hierarchical levels in an organization increases, decisions are decentralized, because centralized decision making would overburden channels of communication.

The assumptions made for purposes of this inquiry cannot be sustained empirically. Personality differences certainly influence organizations, and so do cultural differences. But by studying a large number of organizations, effects of personality differences are randomized, that is, uncorrelated with the critical independent variables. And by studying organizations in one cultural context—the United States—we eliminate societal differences. Rigorous crossnational studies of bureaucracies are needed, but will not be undertaken here. As an analytic procedure, these assumptions are absolutely necessary if one is to understand the mutual interrelations among structural variables that describe organizations. Organizations are not in fact self-contained social systems, but if one wants to study the kinds of issues raised earlier (namely, can bureaucratic structures allow the autonomy and substantial rationality for members?), then one must study organizations as wholes and be content with the unjustifiable, but methodologically crucial, assumption that personality and societal differences can be overlooked.

By deciding to consider only organizational attributes in the present research, the choice of a unit of analysis is determined. To understand interrelations among properties of bureaucratic structures, one must take whole organizations as the unit of analysis. Just what organizations we shall study will be discussed presently.

Perhaps an additional note about organizational structure would be helpful. The notion of structure as used by sociologists and others is

[20]For a discussion of the concepts of effectiveness and efficiency, see Barnard, *Functions of the Executive*, pp. 55-59. The recent literature on effectiveness is summarized in James L. Price, *Organizational Effectiveness* (Homewood, Ill: Irwin, 1968).

very elusive, It sometimes describes recurrent patterns of behavior which are spoken of as structured"[21] it is sometimes identified with beliefs and values which motivate peoples' behavior,[22] and it sometimes refers to properties of groups which have been enacted, or given conscious recognition, by their members.[23] The last, and most concrete, definition of structure is most often used when dealing with organizations. Organizations, compared with other types of groups, are remarkably explicit about the division of responsibilities, the ranking of members, rules and regulations, and goals or immediate objectives to be pursued. The structure of organizations, then, is analytically separable from the behavior of members even though it strongly influences behavior. Rules and regulations, for instance, are obeyed by most people most of the time, but their existence and the fact of obedience are quite different phenomena. Similarly, tables of organization resemble pyramids, at the apex of which are executives who have final authority in all matters. Again, the formal structure and actual decision-making practices are not the same things, for many decisions are delegated to subordinate officials.

The relationship of organizational structure to rationality and authority practices in organizations will be the central focus of this study. We hypothesize that formal organizational structure *does* influence whether or not decisions are made, who makes them, and how more or less predictable behavior is elicited from members. A number of specific propositions will be elaborated in later chapters, but the present task is to lay out the conceptual framework for this inquiry. And the concept of authority needs very close scrutiny.

---

[21]This use of structure figures most prominently in the literature on community decision making. See, for example, Floyd Hunter, *Community Power Structure* (Chapel Hill: University of North Carolina Press, 1953).

[22]Sociological theory tends to identify structure with norms and beliefs, not behavior. See Talcott Parsons, *The Structure of Social Action* (New York: McGraw-Hill, 1937). Parsons tentatively defines sociology as "the science which attempts to develop an analytical theory of social action systems in so far as these systems can be understood in terms of the property of common-value integration" (p. 768). See also Robert K. Merton, "Social Structure and Anomie," in *Social Theory,* pp. 131-160.

[23]William Graham Sumner discusses "enacted" institutions in *Folkways* (Boston: Ginn, 1907), p. 54.

THE TWO FACES OF AUTHORITY

The concept of authority is central to sociological theory.[24] Much of Weber's work is concerned with the development of different bases of legitimate authority and the emergence of new kinds of authority structures, and other theorists have used the concept of authority to examine crossnational differences in industrial organizations.[25] Yet despite the importance of authority in general sociological theory, the concept is persistently used in two diverse and perhaps inconsistent ways. Since the notion of authority is central to the present study, we must be quite explicit about what is meant by it.

The first use of the concept of authority is in the sense of authorization or legitimation of a particular actor to issue commands or obligations that are binding on the other actors in a situation. In this view, authority is an attribute that is attached to specific roles and positions. One who has authority, then, holds it by virtue of his position, and is spoken of as "an authority." The person to whom the commands of an authority are directed is thus the subject of authority.[26] The distinction between authority and subject parallels that between superordinate and subordinate in what is sometimes called an *authority relationship*. Talcott Parsons, among others, has at times advocated this conception of authority:

> Authority is essentially the institutional code within which the use of power as a medium is organized and legitimized. . . . Authority, then, is the aspect of a status in a system of social organization, namely its collective aspect, by virtue of which the incumbent is put in a position legitimately to make decisions which are binding, not only on himself but on the collectivity as a whole and hence its other member-units, in the sense that so far as their implications impinge on their respective role and statuses, they are bound to act in accordance with these implications.[27]

[24] See Robert A. Nisbet, *The Sociological Tradition* (New York: Basic Books, 1966, chap. 4.

[25] See, for example, Reinhard Bendix, *Work and Authority in Industry* (New York: Wiley, 1956).

[26] The distinction between authority and subject is elaborated in Georg Henrik von Wright, *Norm and Action* (London: Routledge and Kegan Paul, 1963), pp. 75-78.

[27] Talcott Parsons, "On the Concept of Political Power," in *Class, Status, Power,* ed. R. Bendix and S. M. Lipset, 2d ed. rev. (New York: Free Press, 1966), p. 249. A similar definition of authority appears in Robert Bierstedt, "The Problem of Authority," in *Freedom and Control in Modern Society,* ed. M. Berger *et al.* (New York: Von Nostrand, 1954), pp. 67-81.

To Parsons, authority legitimates the use of power. Given this conception, one cannot reasonably speak of authority as a social process that occurs between people. Instead, according to Parsons, the relationship between authority and subject must be thought of as the exercise of power, albeit legitimate power.[28] Although this notion of authority as an institutional code that legitimates power jibes very nicely with Weber's notion of bureaucratic authority or authority of the office, it is by no means limited to a bureaucratically structured organization. One may have authority by virtue of his technical competence or expertise. For example, the authority of someone who has professional qualifications derives from his recognized competence.[29] A technical command or directive can be legitimately issued by a person with special qualifications, and it has the same binding power as a directive that emanates from an individual who has authority by virtue of his office.

Parsons also uses the concept of authority to describe some kinds of interpersonal behavior. Authority in this sense is present in the relationship of a supervisor to subordinate in a bureaucracy or doctor to patient in a professional setting. To illustrate: "Authority . . . is a mode of structuring human *relationships* which can be functionally related to the necessity of integrating the activities of many people. . . ."[30] This is from the introduction to Weber's *The Theory of Social and Economic Organization*. Similarly, one would not want to accuse Weber of undue consistency. Although Weber conceives of legal bureaucratic authority as rights and prerogatives accruing to an officeholder, he also speaks of authority as "imperative coordination."[31] Coordination occurs in interpersonal relationships—the behavior of one person is in response to cues given by another—and is not a characteristic of positions or roles. Weber's notion of authority thus includes the element of voluntary submission. Weber recognizes that authority involves normative standards of legitimacy as well as face-to-face interaction between superordinates and subordinates.

---

[28]*Ibid.,* pp. 249-250. Parsons explicitly excludes the use of illegitimate power, that is, coercion, from his analysis.

[29]Talcott Parsons, "Introduction," in Max Weber, *The Theory of Social and Economic Organization,* ed. Talcott Parsons (New York: Oxford University Press, 1947), p. 59.

[30]*Ibid.,* p. 22. (Italics added.)

[31]Weber, *The Theory of Social and Economic Organization,* p. 324.

A second conception of authority involves a complex set of relationships among supervisor, work group, and individual subordinates instead of the simple supervisor-subordinate relationship. Blau argues that the formal authority of a manager is very limited in scope: He can do little more than insist that subordinates perform the tasks assigned them. Blau adds: "Effective management is impossible within the confines of formal authority alone."[32] Authority is then described as something quite different from formal authority of the office. The second kind of authority consists of a manager's exercise of influence as distinct from the formal authority of his office. Although the official prerogatives of a manager are limited, he nonetheless can offer services and rewards to subordinates which in turn obligate subordinates to him. A manager can offer advice and aid because of his superior knowledge; he can offer access to higher-echelon officials; and he can allow exceptions to otherwise binding rules. In sum, a manager can easily do things for subordinates that are not required of him. In return for these services, the obligation of individual subordinates increases. "Every privilege the manager is granted and every rule he is empowered to enforce increase the capital on which he can draw to make subordinates indebted to him."[33] (The reader has perhaps noticed an apparent inconsistency here. Although a manager has "formal authority," it is not the same as the "authority" which emerges from the interaction of managers and subordinates. The difference between the two corresponds exactly to the distinction between authority as authorization or legitimation of a particular role, as Parsons uses the term, and authority as an interpersonal relationship. We shall return to this point presently.)

Blau argues, however, that the development of authority depends on a further transformation. A manager's favors to subordinates produce not only individual, but also collective obligations to him. Subordinates come to believe that the manager's practices contribute to the common good, and shared feelings evolve into group norms which require obedience to managerial directives. Authority relationships are thus the result of a double exchange process: The manager trades favors to his subordinates in return for subordinates' collective obligation to him, and in turn the subordinate peergroup trades social approval in return.

[32]Peter M. Blau, *Exchange and Power in Social Life* (New York: Wiley, 1964), p. 206.
[33]*Ibid.*

for individuals' acceptance of the demands of the manager. "Authority, therefore, rests on the common norms in a collectivity of subordinates that constrain its individual members to conform to the orders of a superior."[34]

Several points about Blau's discussion are very important. First, it recognizes, intentionally or not, the distinction between the different conceptions of authority: authority as rights and prerogatives attached to positions versus authority as interpersonal relationships of super- and subordination.[35] Second, and more important, an empirical relationship between these two forms of authority is posited. In effect, Blau hypothesizes that where someone has authority (i.e., *formal* authority), an authority relationship (i.e., the exercise of influence) between the person with authority and the persons subject to authority emerges through complicated social-psychological processes. That an authority relationship often develops where one person "has authority" in no way obviates the distinction between the two notions of authority, however. Prerogatives attached to individual roles and statuses are altogether different from patterns of interpersonal behavior.

Inevitably, we must ask whether there is a *necessary* connection between the existence of a person or office that has authority and the emergence of an authority relationship characterized by super- and subordination and voluntary compliance on the part of the subordinate. Where the dominant form of authority is the bureaucratic type or authority of the office with formal roles and ranks, such a connection may be inevitable. But there are other forms of authority. One can speak of the authority of custom or tradition, the authority of law, the authority of rules and regulations, and more generally, the authority of institutions. In these cases, it is doubtful that a necessary concomitant of authority is an authority relationship. The legal order is maintained for the most part without overt displays of authority, for example. There would

---

[34]*Ibid.*, p. 208.

[35]We have not discussed the difference between authority and power. Needless to say, so many conceptions of power exist that it would be meaningless to speak of such a difference except in the context of a particular theorist's work. One of the best summaries of the various sources of power is J. R. French, Jr., and B. Raven, "The Bases of Social Power," in *Studies in Social Power*, ed. Dorwin Cartwright (Ann Arbor: Institute for Social Research, 1959), pp. 150-167. French and Raven distinguish reward, coercive, referent, and legitimate power. Their notion of legitimate power comes very close to the use of the term "authority" in this book.

be hardly enough policemen to enforce the law should everyone decide to violate it.

Walter Miller's discussion of authority is illuminating on this point. He describes a society, the Fox Indians, in which there is minimal exercise of authority.

> Even today an observer of Fox society is struck by the fact that organized activity appears to proceed in the absence of any visible authority. A Fox taking part in a fairly large and complex organized enterprise (200-300 people) conducted each year was asked how he knew so well what to do without being told. His answer was, "I just do the same as I did last year. . . ." Thus it was possible for each participant in a collective activity to "control" the plan of action that governed its conduct. He was familiar with the procedural directives specifying the part he was to play and was able to act out these directives without being told what to do. It was as if the action plan for each activity were "built into" each participant.[36]

Miller notes that Fox society maintains order for the most part without a complicated hierarchical structure of command and "higher" and "lower" offices. Each Fox has a definite notion of what he is obligated to do, and he does not require direction from someone else. In effect, the distinction between a person who has authority and a person who is subject to another's authority has disappeared. Any one member of Fox society is simultaneously an authority and subject to his own authority. In one sense, this statement indicates only that most of the Fox have internalized cultural norms governing behavior to the extent that external controls are unnecessary.[37] But in another sense, absence of any distinction between a person with authority and a person subject to authority, between super- and subordinate, reflects the very wide distribution of authority in Fox society. One can think of Fox society,

[36]Walter Miller, "Two Concepts of Authority," *American Anthropologist,* 57, 1955, 285.

[37]See Sigmund Freud's discussion of conscience in *Civilization and Its Discontents,* trans. J. Strachey (New York: Norton, 1961), pp. 83-84. Conscience "is the immediate expression of fear of the external authority, a recognition of the tension between the ego and that authority. It is the direct derivative of the conflict between the need for the authority's love and the urge towards instinctual satisfaction, whose inhibition produces the inclination towards aggression. The superimposition of these two strata of the sense of guilt—one coming from the fear of the *external* authority, the other from fear of *internal* authority—has hampered our insight into the position of conscience in a number of ways."

or any social system in which each member governs his own behavior in pursuit of collective goals without reference to directives of a superior, as an organization in which each member is "authorized" to govern his own conduct. The Fox Indians, of course, are an extreme case of a society in which authority is widely distributed. But it illustrates what may be a general principle of social organization: As authority, in the sense of authorization or legitimation of an actor to impose obligations on others (or himself), is increasingly shared among members of a group, authority relationships that involve super- and subordination become less common. Authority relationships thus typify situations in which few actors have authority relative to the number that do not.

Let us note one more thing about Miller's account. It could be argued that, from the perspective of the individual person or actor, authority among the Fox operates much as it does in a more highly differentiated or bureaucratized society.[38] Since authority is very diffused in Fox society, it could be said that any one member can authoritatively sanction misbehavior of another. Furthermore, anticipation of such sanctions in Fox society guides behavior as effectively as where there are more overt controls. To some extent, this may in fact be the case. But even so, authority relationships characteristic of modern societies are unlikely to appear among the Fox. In the absence of well-established superordinate positions, loyalty of a subordinate group to a single person, and thus his legitimacy as an authority figure, is unlikely to develop.

At this point the definition of authority to be used in this study becomes fairly clear. The notion of authority as a mode of interpersonal behavior is limited to relations between formally designated supervisors and subordinates. As such, it cannot account for patterns of cooperation and informal coordination that occur in organizations where few supervisor-subordinate relationships actually occur, for instance, in organizations with many professional employees. In addition, defining authority as a form of interpersonal behavior excludes some familiar ideas such as the authority of the law or of rules

---

[38]The action frame of reference which views social life from the perspective of the individual actor is discussed in Talcott Parsons *et al.*, "Some Fundamental Categories in the Theory of Action: A General Statement," *Toward a General Theory in Action*, ed. T. Parsons (Cambridge, Mass.: Harvard University Press, 1951), pp. 4-8.

and regulations. Finally, as a practical matter, it is quite difficult to record authority relationships as they actually take place in large organizations. Only by spending several months studying patterns of interaction can an observer describe the exercise of authority within an organization. By contrast, when authority is considered as an attribute of organizational roles or positions, it becomes easy to ascertain authority patterns by asking informants factual questions like, "Who has authority to decide promotions?"

There are other advantages in using this concept of authority. For one, the extent to which an organization allows substantial rationality to its members corresponds closely to the distribution of formal authority within it. The more people who have the prerogative to direct other's work *as well as to decide their own activities,* the greater the amount of discretion that is exercised. (It is sometimes argued that the more bosses, the more bossism, but this assertion will be dealt with presently.) Should only one person in an organization, its head, have authority, substantial rationality as Mannheim defines it is nearly absent. Should many have authority, substantial rationality is increased, and considerably so if some peoples' authority is based on hierarchical position and others' on qualities such as expertness. Another advantage is that the study of actual authority relationships inevitably brings up questions of personality, motivation, and a host of idiosyncratic factors. The importance of social-psychological variables is not denied, but they are deliberately excluded from this analysis for reasons already discussed. If one wants to know what structural conditions promote individual autonomy, his inquiry ought to focus on structures, and not the individual persons who occupy roles within them.

THE STUDY DESIGN

A survey of 254 city, county, and state agencies which have primary responsibility for financial administration in their jurisdictions provided data for this study. Most of these agencies are called departments of finance or comptrollers' offices. All maintain the official financial records of their governments, but most departments have more than bookkeeping responsibilities. Many collect tax revenues; some prepare annual budgets; one runs the county morgue. Finance departments were chosen for this study because there are many of them, and they are larger and more complex than most units of government. In addition, the administration of public funds requires elaborate codes and procedural checks. Weber remarked that the earliest examples of rational bureaucratic organization occurred in offices in charge of public funds.[39]

So varied are the departments of finance that it is difficult to describe a typical one. Some are only accounting offices; responsibility for the budget, collection of funds, and maintenance of the treasury lies elsewhere. At the other extreme, a few departments in addition to their administrative activities direct services such as management of government-owned real estate and operation of parking garages. A number of finance agencies now have their own computers and operate data-processing units that serve other departments. Whether or not the data-processing facilities will remain within finance departments is unclear. Administrative considerations probably weigh against this, but finance directors are quite influential and may wish to retain control of the computer.

The physical settings of these departments are as diverse as their activities. Some are located in buildings that reek with age. (The author stumbled over a spittoon in one.) Others are housed in modern government "campuses" several miles from downtown centers. The quality of finance administration is equally variable if subjective impressions are at all correct. A number of officials were able to provide nearly all the requested information from either memory or desk blotters. Others, by contrast, had little firsthand knowledge of their organizations and were in some cases frankly surprised when confronted with facts brought out by the interviews. When asked about absenteeism, one finance director who headed a department of nearly sixty employees sent his assistant for the attendance records. The following ensued when the assistant returned with the leather-bound ledger:

[39]Weber thought that nonbureaucratic means of finance administration were unlikely to succeed. He writes: "The Roman Latifundia owners liked to commission slaves with the direct management of money matters, because of the possibility of subjecting them to torture. In China, similar results have been sought by the prodigal use of bamboo as a disciplinary instrument. The chances, however, for such direct means of coercion to function with steadiness are extremely unfavorable." See "Bureaucracy," p. 208.

Assistant: Let's see—twelve, twenty, thirty-nine, sixty-one, eighty-four, one hundred eleven—yes, one hundred thirty-seven man-days of absenteeism in March.

Director: My God, that's awful. Why didn't anyone tell me about this?

Needless to say, outbursts like this one were uncommon. This study made no attempt to assess the quality of finance departments, but certain impressions were unavoidable.

The director of finance is often the second most powerful official in local or state government, and recent trends would seem to buttress his position. "Centralized" finance administration is becoming more the rule than the exception. Rather than dividing activities such as accounting, budgeting, purchasing, taxation, and maintenance of the treasury among separate departments, these activities are assigned to units of the larger finance department.[40] In part, an attempt to simplify lines of authority at high levels of government motivates this change, but there is also recognition that various financial activities cannot be separated if they are each to operate efficiently. Figure 1 illustrates the organization of a "centralized" department.

The 254 departments were selected from a list of the chief financial officers of all cities in the United States with populations of 50,000 or more, all counties with populations of 100,000 or more, the fifty states, and the District of Columbia. The Municipal Finance Officers' Association of the United States and Canada compiled this information (their generous help throughout the course of this research is hereby acknowledged). All officials on this list were mailed a questionnaire asking the number of employees, the number of job titles present in their departments, and the names of major subunits (called divisions or bureaus). Over 90 percent of departments which were sent the preliminary mail questionnaires returned them completed. From the results, departments with twenty or more employees and two or more divisions or bureaus were selected for intensive study. Interviews were planned in 263 departments and completed in 254. Information about the 254 departments was obtained from knowledgeable sources, usually the department head, his deputy, and an officer in charge of personnel.

---

[40]Centralization here refers to the concentration of diverse activities under a single director, not necessarily centralization of authority.

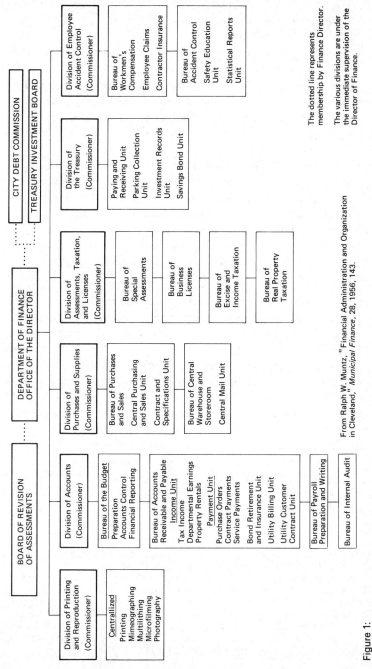

Figure 1:
Organization of a Typical Finance Department

From Ralph W. Muntz, "Financial Administration and Organization in Cleveland," *Municipal Finance*, 28, 1956, 143.

Many of our questions asked for factual and rather precise answers, and interviewers were instructed to seek data from the most qualified informants. Consistency checks were built into the questionnaire so disparate answers could be noted and reconciled. The objective questions included items about the number of employees in the department, the number of job titles, the number of levels of supervision in each branch of the hierarchy, the use of procedure manuals, and so forth. Other questions were asked about various supervisory practices: How much time do supervisors spend directing their subordinates? What are the levels of hierarchy in the department at which different kinds of decisions are made? What are the considerations that govern decisions? The adaptation of survey research techniques to the study of organizational structures was quite successful, and the method is commended to anyone who requires comparable data on large numbers of organizations.

Any questionnaire instrument makes tacit assumptions about the respondent or the unit about which information is sought. For instance, when one asks how many different job titles exist in a finance department, it is assumed that meaningful job titles are present and that different responsibilities are attached to different positions. Similarly, in asking how many levels of supervision exist in an agency, it is assumed that an ordered hierarchy of authority is present. A fixed questionnaire very much limits the range of data that can be collected, but this is the price of having comparable information on many organizations.[41] For instance, from our data there is no direct way to know whether any element of collegiality is present in the administration of finance departments. Certain findings suggest collegiality, but none proves its existence. The reader is asked to bear with some occasionally expansive interpretations which go well beyond what the data alone would justify.

---

[41]Our interview schedule, however, was much less structured than others that have been used in organizational research. The instrument used by the Aston group, for example, arbitrarily classified all employees into six hierarchical levels—above chief executive, whole unit (including chief executive), all workflow activities, workflow subunit, supervisory, and operator. The one measure of vertical differentiation was the number of levels between the executive and operator levels, and here only the longest line of authority was considered rather than an average across lines. See D. S. Pugh *et al.,* "Dimensions of Organizational Structure," *Administrative Science Quarterly,* 13, 1968, 65-105.

PLAN OF THE BOOK

The next chapter deals with the pervasive effects of organizational size. Large organizations increasingly dominate our society, so it seems appropriate to ask whether or not increasing size leads to greater reliance on hierarchical authority to coordinate people's activities. Chapter 3 considers the shape of the hierarchy—short and squat versus tall and thin. Authority practices appear to vary as number of levels and spans of control change. Where lines of communication are extended through proliferation of hierarchical levels, indirect controls in the form of rules and regulations are substituted for centralized decision making. The fourth chapter examines some effects of automation which is often a source of conflict between those who understand the computer and those who do not, but depend on it. Chapter 5 considers the impact of self-containment and expertness on organizational units. With increasing self-containment of organizational subunits, other changes occur which suggest upward communication or feedback. The last chapter summarizes the findings, asks whether they can be generalized to all organizations, and returns to the question of individual autonomy and rationality in bureaucratic settings.

2
Some Effects of Organizational Size

SIZE AS A THEORETICAL CONCEPT

The size of an organization, or of any group, affects both its internal structure and its behavior toward outsiders. Sociological theory has long recognized the distinction between small and large groups. The former usually have less than twenty members who know one another by name, communicate freely, and rely on one or two people to act as leaders without designating them as such when faced with a common task. In large-scale organizations, by contrast, members may be only cursorily acquainted, communication is often in writing, and formal statuses or positions determine in advance who has the right to give directions. Social control in small groups operates through collective norms and expressions of disapproval; in cases of extreme misbehavior, ostracism is the ultimate sanction. Organizations usually have detailed rules and regulations which are meant to guide people's behavior, and specific penalties such as loss of rank or pay may be incurred when violations are detected.[1]

Economists have also recognized several implications of increasing organizational size. For one thing, size is said to promote economies of scale. As production of a commodity increases, standardized work

---

[1]Groups organized for "the explicit purpose of achieving certain goals" are usually called "formal organizations." I prefer to distinguish organizations from other groups in terms of their structural characteristics. The purposive nature of organizations is emphasized in Peter M. Blau and W. Richard Scott, *Formal Organizations* (San Francisco: Chandler, 1962), pp. 5-8.

processes which lower labor costs develop along with more efficient utilization of plant and materials. Domination of a market which is the concomitant of growth also produces oligopolistic conditions. A paucity of sellers renders buyers nearly powerless; likewise, a limited number of buyers, oligopsony, jeopardizes a seller's chance of getting reasonable prices for his goods.[2] Some sociologists have used these basic principles of economics to construct arguments about organizational (as contrasted with economic) processes. It is said, for example, that organizations continually strive to expand, at least until the least reducible component is fully utilized.[3] It is also said that expansion renders individual people powerless, removing not only opportunities for substantial rationality as Mannheim envisioned, but also concentrating political and economic influence in the hands of a small elite of politicians, generals, and executives.[4]

There is a possible inconsistency between the notion that organizational structure changes dramatically with size and the notion that increasing size makes organizations more powerful. To be sure, as "informal organizations" (to use Chester Barnard's phrase) of only two or three members are transformed into large formal organizations, a hierarchy of authority and elaborate administrative codes are likely to emerge. They are needed to ensure more or less predictable behavior and prompt execution of managers' orders, for lacking such devices no one knows who is in charge or what are the bounds of acceptable conduct. In this sense, large organizations are apt to rely on the use of formal authority in place of informal persuasion. The question raised in this chapter is whether some of the mechanisms intended to maintain order and authority in bureaucracies lose effectiveness as organizations grow even larger. In particular, we shall ask whether maintenance of a rigid hierarchy of authority, and of "strict super- and subordination" to quote Weber, and the absence of discretion to make meaningful decisions become quite clumsy when organizations expand beyond even modest size. Critics who equate growth of organizations with concentration of power deny this, assuming implicitly that a high degree of predictability and control is possible in large organizations just as in

---

[2]That is, unless prices are otherwise fixed, rigged, or set by cartels.

[3]James D. Thompson, *Organizations in Action* (New York: McGraw-Hill, 1967), p. 46.

[4]See, for example, C. Wright Mills, *The Power Elite* (New York: Oxford University Press, 1959).

small ones. But it may be that the same variable, organizational size, which appears to increase the power of organizations also limits their capacity to dominate and control their members' lives.

Remarkably little attention has been paid to group size in sociological research. In part, this reflects the concern with attitudes and beliefs which has pervaded empirical studies. The sample survey overlooks group properties by asking questions of individual persons but ignoring relations among them. Where variables describing groups have been considered, they usually measure the predominant social characteristics of a collection of people (for example, their median income) or predominant attitudes (for example, the "climate of opinion" in a community). Research on organizations has not been immune from this tendency either. A recent study of several business firms treats the divergent attitudes among employees as indicative of high differentiation, confounding the distinction between differences in workers' outlooks and differences in formal structure which may or may not have existed together.[5]

Sociological theory also shares the blame for overlooking size as a key variable. Many theorists prefer to regard sociology as a conceptual science which deals with abstractions such as community, authority, status, alienation, and the like.[6] The notion of size is hardly abstract; indeed, it is so immediate and concrete as to be unappealing as a central variable in a theoretical scheme. Much, therefore, is made of the distinction between small groups, organizations, communities, and nation-states, but differences between groups are usually attributed to their purposes and functions rather than to variations in size. Organizations, for instance, are said to have specific objectives whereas small groups do not. Formal hierarchies of authority and other control mechanisms therefore appear in organizations whereas informal groups lack these. The fact that organizations are often several orders of magnitude larger than small groups is noted, but size is not causally

[5]Paul R. Lawrence and Jay W. Lorsch, *Organization and Environment* (Boston: Harvard Business School, Division of Research, 1967), pp. 30-39. Three of four measures of differentiation are interpersonal orientations of workers, time orientations, and goal orientations. Variation in formal structure is the fourth measure.

[6]See, for example, Robert A. Nisbet, *The Social Bond* (New York: Knopf, 1970), pp. 84-97, for a refreshing exception to this. I was unable to find any reference to group size in a number of other sociology texts.

associated with formalization of purposes and procedures. Rather, the association is viewed as a matter of happenstance. Communities, similarly, are distinguished from organizations by virtue of their peculiar functions. The *Encyclopedia of Social Sciences* defines a community as "a territorially bounded social system or set of interlocking or integrated functional subsystems . . . serving a resident population plus the material culture or physical plant through which the subsystems operate."[7] Again, the size of communities compared to organizations is treated as incidental. Certainly there are some very large organizations which barely resemble bureaucracies as Weber saw them, for example, the Boy Scouts of America. There are also tiny organizations of less than a half dozen members. But if one stripped the label "organization" from groups with explicit and limited purposes, he would probably find that the smallest ones are little different from informal groups. And the largest organizations would in all likelihood resemble collections of organizations with independent and occasionally conflicting interests, not much different from communities as described above.

Where sociological theory has considered effects of group size, it has done so obliquely and usually as an ecological variable. Durkheim's *The Division of Labor in Society* comes closest to using size as an explanatory variable, but the term "moral density" appears instead. As large numbers of people settle in a limited area, communication and transportation are eased. Specialization of roles thus becomes possible, relationships of interdependence emerge, and reciprocity substitutes for repressive means of social control.

> The division of labor develops, therefore, as there are more individuals sufficiently in contact to be able to act and react upon one another. If we agree to call this relation and the active commerce resulting from it dynamic or moral density, we can say that the progress of the division of labor is in direct ratio to the moral or dynamic density of society.
>
> But this moral relationship can only produce its effect if the real distance between individuals has itself diminished in some way. Moral density cannot grow unless material density grows at the same time, and the latter can be used to measure the former.[8]

[7]Jessie Bernard, "Community Disorganization," in *International Encyclopedia of the Social Sciences*, vol. 3 (New York: Macmillan, 1968), p. 163.
[8]Emile Durkheim, *The Division of Labor in Society* (New York: Macmillan, 1933), p. 257.

Marx, by contrast, foresaw different consequences of agglomeration of population. Class consciousness, the awareness of a common situation and common grievances, develops as workers are brought together in large factories and shops. So long as its members are scattered, the proletariat exists only as an abstract category of people who share similar material circumstances, according to Marx. Industrialization, particularly large-scale capitalist enterprises, concentrates the proletariat in workshops and urban neighborhoods. Understanding of their collective plight and the transformation of false consciousness into class consciousness occur because of the sheer number of workers brought together; a situation conducive to militancy is created.

> The advance of industry, whose involuntary promoter is the bourgeoisie, replaces the isolation of laborers, due to competition, by their revolutionary combination due to association. The development of modern industry, therefore, cuts from under its feet the very foundation on which the bourgeoisie produces and appropriates products. What the bourgeoisie, therefore, produces, above all, is its own gravediggers.[9]

Durkheim's and Marx's analyses are alike in one respect: Both conclude that the rate of interaction between people increases with group size. Between size and its effects (reciprocity or class consciousness) intervene intensive interchanges that lead to shared beliefs and experiences (with interdependence or class antagonisms). Indeed, one might imagine that as the size of any group increases, so does the density of interaction because there are so many more people with whom to talk. If frequency of interaction is ignored, one finds that the number of possible links or connections between members of fully interconnected groups increases much faster than size. In a group of n individuals, the maximum number of links is $\frac{1}{2}n(n-1)$. (A fully interconnected group is illustrated in Figure 2.) Bureaucracies, indeed most organizations, are not fully interconnected groups, and some may limit communication to formally designated superiors and subordinates. A hierarchical structure assigns to each member one and only one superior so that the number of links in an organization of n persons is $n-1$; density of interaction does not increase with size. (Figure 2 also shows a typical hierarchy.) The effects of size on other group properties

[9]Karl Marx, "Manifesto of the Communist Party," in *Marx and Engels: Basic Writings on Politics and Philosophy,* ed. Lewis S. Feuer (Garden City, N.Y.: Doubleday, 1959), pp. 19-20.

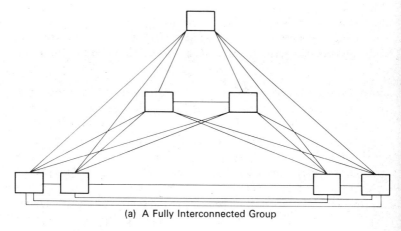

(a) A Fully Interconnected Group

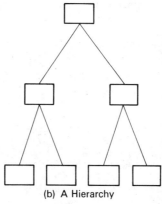

(b) A Hierarchy

Figure 2
Fully Interconnected and Hierarchical Groups

also

thus depends to some extent on whether or not a hierarchical structure is maintained. If an organization adheres to traditional assumptions about hierarchy and subordination, increasing size only extends lines of communication, adds to the number of workers reporting to each supervisor, or both. If not, the inverted tree structure of offices gives way to something else, perhaps disaggregation of one large structure into several small ones among which only tenuous connections exist, or perhaps a collegial pattern where there are horizontal ties. Indeed, both of these developments can occur simultaneously: A hierarchical organization can divide into several smaller units within which collegial relations prevail. But the effects of disaggregation and collegiality are likely to be quite different. The former, if anything, decreases communication between people, while the latter promotes interaction and thus group consciousness and cohesion as described by Durkheim and Marx.

Organizational theory has likewise had relatively little to say about the concomitants of size. And there has been little research on how size affects mechanisms of hierarchical control and coordination.[10] Studies have dealt with the relationship of size to the administrative, clerical, or overhead components of organizations, but their results have been inconclusive.[11] The work of Blau and his colleagues has led to a theory of differentiation in organizations in which size is the key variable, but the theory has been the subject of some dispute.[12] Research of the Aston group has shown size to be an important predictor of many variables describing organizational structure, but relatively little attention was paid to the implications of these findings.[13] The absence of

[10]An important exception is Richard H. Hall, J. Eugene Haas, and Norman J. Johnson, "Organizational Size, Complexity, and Formalization," *American Sociological Review,* 32, 1967, 903-912.

[11]See, for example, Frederic W. Terrien and Donald L. Mills, "The Effect of Changing Size upon the Internal Structure of Organizations," *American Sociological Review,* 20, 1955, 11-13; Theodore R. Anderson and Seymour Warkov, "Organizational Size and Functional Complexity: A Study of Administration in Hospitals," *American Sociological Review,* 26, 1961, 23-28; William H. Starbuck, "Organizational Growth and Development," in *Handbook of Organizations,* ed. James G. March (Chicago: Rand McNally, 1965), pp. 451-533.

[12]Peter M. Blau and Richard A. Schoenherr, *The Structure of Organizations* (New York: Basic Books, 1970); Peter M. Blau, "A Formal Theory of Differentiation in Organizations," *American Sociological Review,* 35, 1970, 201-218. See also Marshall W. Meyer, "Constraints in Analyzing Data on Organizational Structures," *American Sociological Review,* 36, 1971, 293-297.

[13]D. S. Pugh *et al.,* "The Context of Organizational Structures," *Administrative Science Quarterly,* 14, 1969, 91-114.

theory or research findings relating size to authority practices makes it somewhat difficult to test specific hypotheses here. We can only state some general notions which relate size to variables describing coordination and control in bureaucratic organizations. It would be misleading to give the appearance of testing specific propositions which are part of a body of theory which does not exist. One general notion is that large organizations are more bureaucratic, rigid, and centralized, and therefore more dehumanizing than small ones. Opposed to it is the notion that increasing size compels fundamental changes in administrative processes which render large organizations less structured and dominating than small ones. Put another way, the second notion says that growth reduces rather than enhances the importance of hierarchy, subordination, and the chain of command. Neither of these notions, it turns out, is altogether correct among departments of finance, but we shall let the data lead us to specific hypotheses rather than the other way around.

SIZE AND FORMAL STRUCTURE

The use of a questionnaire to gather comparable data on a large number of organizations required some assumptions about finance departments that may not have been wholly realistic. Whether or not hierarchical distinctions were observed in practice, informants answered questions as if they were. Department heads were asked to list division heads and others at the second level of hierarchy; division heads in turn identified their immediate subordinates, the people who reported to these subordinates, and so on until the nonsupervisory level was reached. Some departments had as few as three layers of hierarchy, while one claimed ten intermediate levels between the lowest and highest offices. How many of these intermediate levels actually perform supervisory functions is a moot question, however. A multilevel hierarchy can be designed to satisfy administrative considerations: Everyone is placed in a neat chain of command, even though some people who nominally hold supervisory posts do little or no supervising. The dilemma in this research was whether or not to accept division heads' descriptions of the hierarchy as the actual structure of an organization. To do this introduces some possible inaccuracies into the data, especially in larger divisions and departments, but not to do so creates other problems. One strategy is to define in advance various categories of management—executive, senior administrative, other administrative with supervisory responsibility, administrative without supervisory responsibility, and so forth—and fit all employees above the lowest level into these. This procedure has the virtue of distinguishing true supervisors from people who are supervisors in name only, but it precludes consideration of the number of levels of hierarchy, real or imagined, as a variable in analyzing organizational structures.[14] Another possibility is to observe people's behavior in organizations and construct a realistic hierarchy from such data. Were it not for limited time and funds, this would have been the ideal procedure. But since the task was to study a large number of organizations in something less than a decade, this was out of the question.

Given the assumption that finance departments are hierarchically organized, one can anticipate that structural differentiation will intensify with size. Indeed, this is implicit in the definition of hierarchy. New members of an organization must be placed alongside, above, or below others. Increased spans of control (the ratio of subordinates to supervisors) or levels of hierarchy or both necessarily follow. Some of the data in Table 1 are therefore hardly surprising. As Table 1 indicates, the smallest bureaucracies have fewer levels of hierarchy, divisions, and sections within divisions than others. Moreover, spans of control are narrowest in small departments. Just the opposite holds in the largest departments with more than one hundred members. (The largest department has 1712 full-time employees, but only a handful have more than three hundred.) They have more levels, divisions, and sections than others, and spans of control are widest in them. In general, size is conducive to structural differentiation both vertically through multiplication of ranks and horizontally through increasing numbers of subunits, sections, and offices.

More interesting comparisons can be made by reading down the columns of Table 1 rather than across the rows. Departments with twenty to thirty-four employees, the smallest ones in this study, have a mean of 4.41 operating divisions whose heads report to the head of the department. The mean span of control of lowest-level supervisors is about the same, 4.45, and the average number of hierarchical levels is 3.50. All the 254 finance departments have at least three levels: department head, division head, and nonsupervisory employee. Thus,

---

[14]The Aston group used essentially this procedure. It is described in footnote 41, chap. 1.

Table 1
Structural Differentiation by Size (Means and Standard Errors)

| | Number of Employees | | | |
	20-34	35-59	60-99	100+
Levels of Hierarchy	3.50	3.64	3.96	4.68
Error	0.08	0.07	0.09	0.13
N	(64)	(64)	(64)	(62)
Operating Divisions	4.41	5.28	5.67	7.90
Error	0.22	0.20	0.27	0.47
N	(64)	(64)	(64)	(62)
Number of Sections*	6.65	9.45	10.53	21.77
Error	0.35	0.87	0.44	1.62
N	(64)	(64)	(64)	(62)
Span of Control of First-Line Supervisors	4.45	5.49	7.13	11.55
Error	0.28	0.36	0.37	0.93
N	(64)	(64)	(64)	(61)
Span of Control of Intermediate Supervisors	1.36	1.60	1.81	2.09
Error	0.11	0.10	0.13	0.09
N	(56)	(57)	(61)	(61)

*If a division is not formally divided into sections, it is counted as one section.

the mean of 3.50 levels indicates that most divisions of small departments have no supervisory positions below the level of division heads who are thus first-line supervisors. Where intermediate levels of hierarchy are present in small departments, spans of control of division heads drop to 1.36, much lower than spans of control of either department heads or first-line supervisors. A similar pattern holds among larger departments. The spans of control of department heads, intermediate supervisors, and first-line supervisors are, respectively, 5.28, 1.60, and 5.49 in departments with thirty-five to fifty-nine employees, 5.67, 1.81, and 7.13 where there are sixty to ninety-nine employees, and 7.90, 2.09, and 11.55 in departments with one hundred or more members. The formal *structure* of supervision at intermediate levels of finance departments is very different from what takes place at the highest and lowest ranks. Regardless of size, the ratio of subordinates to supervisors is much lower at intermediate levels than elsewhere.

The largest organizations tend to have more intermediate layers of supervision than small departments. Finance agencies with more than one hundred members have a mean of 4.68 grades of hierarchy, meaning that almost all their divisions have one level of supervision between division heads and operating employees, and many have more than one such level. Increasing organizational size, therefore, is accompanied by proliferation of intermediate levels at which spans of control are very low. (This finding, it should be noted, is not an artifact of the assumption that finance departments are hierarchically organized.) Growth compels both vertical and horizontal differentiation of organizations, but the distinctive feature of large finance departments compared with small ones is the number of middle managers who have very few subordinates. The effects of size on structural differentiation in organizations may thus be summarized as follows: Increasing size leads to greater horizontal differentiation at the second level of hierarchy (that of division heads) and at the lowest level. Size also promotes horizontal differentiation at intermediate levels and significantly so, but the relative growth in spans of control (from 1.36 to 2.09) is much less than the increase in intermediate levels (from 0.50 to 1.68).

The structures of small and large finance departments are illustrated in Figure 3. The small organization in Figure 3 (a) has three levels of hierarchy and spans of control of four throughout; the number of positions increases geometrically from top to bottom. In the large organization this geometric increase does not hold. In the model (which exaggerates the distinctive attributes of large organizations), there are no more people at the third level of hierarchy than at the second; the span of control of division heads is one. Spans of control at the highest and lowest levels are, by contrast, eight. If formal structures of organizations reflect people's behavior as they must to some extent, it appears that relationships of intermediate supervisors to their subordinates are very different from those that take place at other levels of organizations.

For the present, we can only speculate about the nature of this difference. Let us suppose that, at least in large departments, wide spans of control characterize *working units,* groups where the distinction between boss and subordinates is maintained and tangible problems are handled. The organization illustrated in Figure 3 (b) would include working units at different levels: one consisting of the department head and his immediate subordinates, and eight others consisting of first-line supervisors and operating employees. Let us

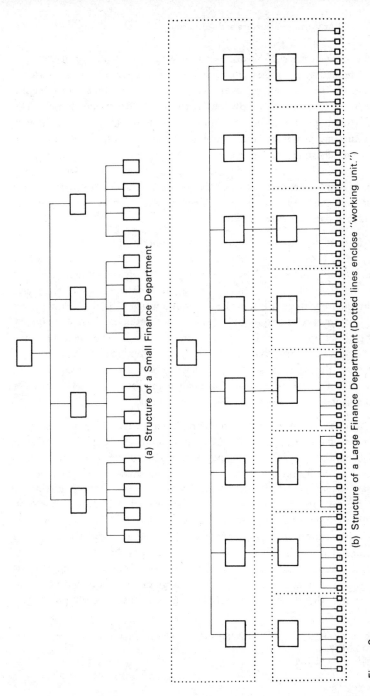

(a) Structure of a Small Finance Department

(b) Structure of a Large Finance Department (Dotted lines enclose "working unit.")

Figure 3
Structures of Small and Large Departments

make some further suppositions about what the working units actually do. The activities of first-line supervisors and their subordinates are no mystery. They are an organization's "work," the pursuit of concrete operational goals, to adopt the language of March and Simon. The department head and division chiefs are probably most concerned with formulating programs and defining responsibilities, developing non-operational goals, to follow March and Simon.[15] What takes place between division heads and first-line supervisors is less clear. Let me tentatively suggest that this is the point where the translation from nonoperational to operational objectives, the conversion of abstract ends into concrete means, takes place.

To transform nonoperational goals into operational ones is no simple matter. It is certainly more complex than ordering subordinates about and probably more so than developing overall organizational objectives in the first place. Where the tasks of identifying objectives and implementing them are separated, communication between supervisors and different working units is necessarily intense. Narrow spans of control are appropriate because so much effort is devoted to planning and specifying procedures. To be sure, differences of rank remain between the various supervisory levels, but the high frequency of interaction between levels and the small number of subordinates per supervisor suggest that they are not very salient.

We now have a hypothesis connecting organizational size with patterns of coordination and control. Large bureaucracies, it is argued, distin-guish nonoperational from operational goals, policies from procedures, whereas small organizations lack mechanisms to do this. Large organizations develop intermediate levels of supervision to effect the transformation from nonoperational to operational goals; these posi-tions are usually absent from small organizations. The hypothesis, it should be noted, does not emerge directly from the work of March and Simon. The authors of *Organizations* assert that all bureaucratic systems reduce abstract objectives to concrete operations.[16] This statement, our data suggest, holds for large organizations but not small ones. For the latter, the department head alone may set policy and

---

[15]James G. March and Herbert A. Simon, *Organizations* (New York: Wiley, 1958), pp. 155-157.
[16]*Ibid.*, pp. 151-154.

decide how it is to be carried out; any distinction between operational and nonoperational goals is indeed tenuous. But more direct data are needed at this point.

SIZE AND SUPERVISORY PRACTICES

The hypothesis could be easily confirmed or disconfirmed if we had detailed information about the activities of supervisors. Such data are unfortunately lacking, and a roundabout path will have to be taken. Informants were asked about actual supervisory practices in divisions of finance departments. For each level of hierarchy except the lowest, the proportion of time employees at that level spend supervising others was estimated. Supervision was defined very broadly. It included, according to the specifications which guided interviewers, "time spent in directing, reviewing, or planning other employees' work, including personnel reports, assignments, all administrative details related to personnel, and policy matters which affect the division." After the fact, it is clear that time spent directing other people's work should have been separated from planning, reviewing, and policy matters. The data are less than ideal for present purposes.

If the estimates of time spent supervising are at all accurate, managers devote about forty percent of their effort to directing, planning, or reviewing the work of others; the remainder is taken by their "own" work. In finance departments it is quite common for supervisors to do essentially the same jobs as the people who report to them—approving disbursements, auditing, budgeting, and so forth. Supervisors must approve of items involving large sums of money, and discrepancies or irregularities detected by subordinates are always brought to their attention. Managerial positions in finance departments, and perhaps public bureaucracies generally, are thus very different from supervisory positions in industrial settings.[17] The need for a "straw boss" or

[17] For an account of a factory setting, see, for example, Charles R. Walker *et al.*, *The Foreman on the Assembly Line* (Cambridge, Mass.: Harvard University Press, 1956). In a sense we have introduced the variable of technology here. Bureaucracies do essentially administrative tasks which, while more or less routine, are neither nearly so standardized nor so governed by an inexorable work flow as are manufacturing tasks in industry. Hence, bureaucratic supervisors are required to have considerable technical competence which enables subordinates to

Table 2
Supervisory Practices by Size (Means and Standard Errors)

	Number of Employees			
	20-34	35-59	60-99	100+
Proportion of Time First-Line				
Supervisors Supervise	0.339	0.336	0.393	0.371
Error	0.025	0.025	0.024	0.021
N	(64)	(63)	(64)	(60)
Proportion of Time Intermediate				
Supervisors Supervise	0.435	0.426	0.492	0.494
Error	0.036	0.031	0.025	0.023
N	(56)	(56)	(61)	(60)
Highest Level Where Maximum				
Supervision Occurs	2.04	2.11	2.22	2.45
Error	0.032	0.040	0.037	0.062
N	(64)	(63)	(64)	(60)
Lowest Level Where Maximum				
Supervision Occurs	2.22	2.30	2.35	2.79
Error	0.064	0.047	0.047	0.078
N	(64)	(64)	(64)	(60)
Proportion of Total Effort				
Devoted to Supervision	0.107	0.091	0.097	0.087
Error	0.008	0.006	0.005	0.005
N	(64)	(63)	(64)	(60)

"pusher" who actively coordinates work is not great in bureaucracies, but the kind of technical competence Weber spoke of, detailed knowledge of regulations and procedures, is important. One also suspects that good judgment, if not a bit of political savvy, can be very helpful to managers.

In Table 2 we note that supervisors in large departments spend more of their time actually supervising than do their counterparts in small organizations. The differences are not great, however. In the smallest departments, for example, about 34 percent of the effort of first-line supervisors is spent on directing, planning, or reviewing the work of others; this increases to about 37 percent in the largest finance agencies. Greater differences appear at intermediate levels; the proportions of

seek supervisors' advice, and allows the latter greater responsibilities (for example, authority to approve vouchers for large sums of money). Leadership qualities and sheer ambition may be more important in industry; see, for example, Eli Chinoy, *Automobile Workers and the American Dream* (New York: Random House, 1955).

time spent supervising range from about 43 percent in the smallest to 49 percent in the largest departments. In large organizations which have wider spans of control, and thus proportionally fewer managers than small ones, supervisors have somewhat more supervising to do than elsewhere. The more subordinates, the more directing, planning, and reviewing of work is required. But a different pattern emerges if comparisons are made within organizations rather than between them. Despite the very narrow spans of control at intermediate levels, the proportion of time spent supervising at that level is much greater than at the operating level of organizations. In the smallest finance departments, for example, spans of control at the lowest and intermediate levels are 4.45 and 1.36, respectively, while the estimates of time spent supervising are 34 and 44 percent. In the largest departments, spans of control of 11.55 and 2.09 are associated with time estimates of 37 and 49 percent. If managers at the various levels had similar responsibilities, this pattern would not be expected. Apparently, the activities of intermediate supervisors include considerably more planning and reviewing of others' work than occur at lower levels.

Possibly informants did not give interviewers correct information, but whether or not they systematically biased their estimates of supervisory effort is another matter. There may have been a tendency to attribute greater supervisory duties to higher supervisors on the assumption that responsibility is commensurate with rank. Some of the data in Table 2 weigh against this possibility, however. The third and fourth rows of the table show the levels of hierarchy at which the greatest proportion of time is devoted to supervision within divisions of finance departments. The third row differs slightly from the fourth because of ties occurring when supervisors at different levels spent equal amounts of time supervising. The means in the third row were computed by counting the highest (numerically the lowest) level when ties occurred; means in the fourth row were computed by counting the lowest (numerically the highest) level when different levels devoted equal effort to supervision. But regardless of how one computes the level where maximum supervision occurs, this level is somewhat (and significantly) lower in large departments than in small ones. The figures in the third row are the most conservative estimates of the extent to which someone other than the division head has major supervisory responsibility. In the smallest departments, the mean level of maximum supervision is 2.04, indicating that in practically all cases division heads spend more time planning, directing, and reviewing the work than others. By contrast, the mean level of maximum supervision rises to 2.45 in the largest departments. In many, though not a majority of them, the greatest amount of supervision occurs a level or two below division heads. And if one counts the lowest instead of the highest levels in cases of ties, the mean level of maximum supervision becomes 2.79 in the largest departments. In other words, most finance departments with one hundred or more employees have supervisors below the level of division heads who spend as much or more or their time supervising than anyone else. These data make it appear unlikely that informants systematically biased their estimates of supervisory effort to make it appear that higher managers were indeed supervising more than others.

Earlier we hypothesized that large organizations separate nonoperational from operational goals whereas small organizations do not. Let us now summarize the data presented so far. These findings are consistent with the hypothesis though they do not necessarily prove it.

1. Large organizations have more intermediate levels of hierarchy than small ones.
2. Spans of control are quite narrow at intermediate levels.
3. Yet, intermediate supervisors spend considerably more time supervising than first-line supervisors.

Intermediate supervisors, then, supervise more but have fewer direct subordinates than first-line managers. It will be remembered that the definition of supervision was quite broad, including giving directions, planning, reviewing, and work on policy matters. One might reasonably assume that, lacking many subordinates, intermediate supervisors spend little time directing others' work. Planning, reviewing, and work on policy must constitute most of the supervision they do. This is what would be expected of supervisors at intermediate levels in organizations where long-term objectives are separated from the day-to-day activities of members.

A Note on the Shifting Pattern of Supervision

Supervisors spend more time supervising in large organizations than in small ones partly because they have more subordinates, and partly because more of them are at intermediate levels where attention to planning, review, and policy matters is great. One might imagine that a greater proportion of employees' time is consumed by supervisory duties, broadly defined, in large departments than in small ones, but this is hardly the case. The data in the fifth row of Table 2 indicate that nearly 11 percent of man-hours is devoted to supervision, that is, planning, directing, or reviewing the work of others, in the smallest departments, while this proportion drops to less than 9 percent in the largest agencies. The higher ratio of subordinates to supervisors that accompanies growth more than compensates for increased supervisory duties.

To say that size promotes economies in supervision is probably an oversimplification. Several steps may intervene between increased size and the declining proportion of effort consumed by supervisory duties. Adding employees at the lowest level increases an organization's size and spans of control of first-line supervisors, and thus reduces the proportion of supervisory personnel. But greater size compels separation of nonoperational from operational goals, we would argue, because there is the need to provide new members with specific operational programs of behavior without at the same time overburdening top managers with the task of devising them. This in turn leads to development of intermediate levels of supervision which adds to overall supervisory effort. In finance departments, at least, expanding size is accompanied by economies in supervision, but there is no reason to believe that this holds in all organizations. In organizations whose objectives are diffuse and occasionally conflicting, churches and universities, for example, it may well be that increasing size creates complexities which decrease economies in supervision. Conversely, organizations with simple objectives may expand indefinitely without adding to administrative overhead.[18] These conjectures, in any case, should be tested through empirical research where variables such as complexity of goals and the extent to which nonoperational objectives are separated from operational ones are measured and controlled.

---

[18]This might be stated differently: Large organizations must simplify objectives in order to maintain administrative efficiency. Such simplification occurs when self-contained units replace interdependent ones. See Chapter 5.

SIZE AND CENTRALIZATION OF AUTHORITY

The two general notions about the effects of organizational size—one which associates growth with rigidity and "bureaucracy" in the worst sense of the word, and the other which implies the opposite—also yield predictions about decision-making processes. If large size promotes inflexibility and reliance on hierarchical authority as the primary means of control, then decisions ought to be more centralized in large organizations than in small ones. Social-psychological theories would support this notion; George Homans' discussion of the mutual impact of interaction and similarity of activities on the emergence of collective sentiments, for example, clearly posits pressures toward consensus in small groups.[19] Large hierarchically structured organizations very much limit opportunities for interaction as we have already shown. Social-psychological theory would predict rather weak consensual norms in such groups, and one might expect centralized decision making in place of them. By contrast, if growth leads to movement away from traditional notions of hierarchy and chain of command, some delegation of decision-making authority to lower ranks seems inevitable. No formal theory supports this notion. But, the impression one gets from examining any organization chart suggests that centralized control becomes very cumbersome in large, multilayer organizations. Whatever benefits accrue from centralization are more than lost by the effort expended in funneling information up the hierarchy and decisions down it, and in compensating for the inevitable delays and mistakes made under such circumstances.

The actual pattern of decision making in finance departments gives credence to both notions or theories. Table 3 shows a cross-tabulation of the decision-making authority of division heads by size. Among the smallest departments about half allow division heads discretion over their budgets or accounting procedures; this proportion drops to 34 percent among departments with thirty-five to fifty-nine employees. Very small bureaucracies, it appears, are more likely to delegate authority than those slightly larger. Past this point, however, greater size leads to decentralization. Forty-four percent of departments with sixty to ninety-nine employees and 58 percent with one hundred or

---

[19]George C. Homans, *The Human Group* (New York: Harcourt Brace Jovanovich, 1950), especially pp. 448-449.

Table 3
Authority of Division Heads to Make Decisions by Size

	Size			
	20-34	35-59	60-99	100+
Decisions Delegated to Division Heads				
Work assignments only	51%	66%	56%	42%
Work assignments and other decisions	49	34	44	58
N	(51)	(55)	(54)	(48)

more members allow division heads authority over budgeting and accounting procedures.[20] These data suggest, though hardly prove, a similarity between very small bureaucracies and small groups. Frequent interaction in small organizations gives rise to shared beliefs about what constitutes appropriate and inappropriate conduct; formal centralization of authority is unneccessary where consensus exists on matters pertinent to the organization's work. Slightly larger organizations, in this case departments with thirty-five or more members, cannot maintain consistent standards through informal means, so centralized control emerges and is feasible so long as lines of communication remain relatively short. With even further growth, however, lines of communication are stretched and continued centralization becomes awkward, if not inefficient. A decentralized pattern again emerges at this point, but, as we shall see in the next chapter, it is accompanied by other mechanisms to ensure decisions which are consistent and consonant with organizational goals.

These findings illustrate that the distinction between social-psychological theories which describe people's behavior in relatively small groups and theories of organization which focus on structural attributes of large groups is more than academic. If the data reported in Table 3 are representative of all organizations, it appears that social-psychological propositions hold for small groups whereas structural (or organizational) propositions hold for large ones. Fundamental notions of

[20]Other indicators of centralization of decision-making authority showed similar relationships to size. They will be discussed in the next chapter.

social psychology suggest that small bureaucracies will be least centralized; consideration of basic variables in organization theory such as the number of levels of hierarchy yields the opposite prediction. Both hunches turn out to be correct, but only when applied to the units for which they are appropriate. Neither, in other words, holds for all situations. Reductionism, whether in attempts to generalize about large groups from psychological principles or in efforts to use broad sociological notions to anticipate interpersonal behavior, cannot yield satisfactory results because the different theories apply to groups of different sizes.

SIZE AND THE RATIONALITY OF ORGANIZATIONS

At this point the impact of organizational size on the possibility for individual rationality in bureaucratic settings should be considered. The data are by no means unequivocal on this point. If anything, they suggest that the changes accompanying increased size improve the chances for substantial rationality for some people but diminish them for others. Greater size, we have surmised, leads to separation of nonoperational from operational goals and the emergence of inter-mediate supervisors whose job is to translate vague objectives into specific programs of behavior. Managers at intermediate levels do not act simply on the basis of goals set for them by others. Rather, they must reconcile objectives, which as often as not are ideals beyond realization, with available talents and resources. Through this process, organizational goals themselves are often modified. Intermediate managers thus are able to bring their own insights and values to bear in their work, for they are as much involved in determining objectives as anyone else.

The same does not hold for nonsupervisory employees of large organizations. Increasing size multiplies supervisory positions at intermediate levels where goals are set for others, implying that there are others for whom goals are set. The largest bureaucracies carefully plan the work of members at the lowest ranks, so much so that the chances for substantial rationality for them may be less than in small organizations. A curious equilibrium is thus maintained as organizations grow: The need to use one's "insight into the interrelations of events" is increased for some but diminished for many. Bureaucratization thus serves as the agent of both functional and substantial rationalization, the former for workers at the lowest levels of hierarchy, perhaps the masses Mannheim had in mind, the latter for their managers.

In any case, the formal structures of finance departments as well as actual supervisory practices vary considerably with size. "Strict super- and subordination," which is a central feature of Weber's model of bureaucracy, apparently does not hold at all levels of organizations. Our suspicion is that fairly small, though not the smallest, bureaucracies best fit Weber's model. Large organizations, if the finance departments are representative of them, do not have rigid chains of command running from top to bottom. Instead, they consist of groups which set goals (the head and his immediate subordinates), groups which carry out day-to-day activities (first-line supervisors and their subordinates), and people between these groups whose task is to translate broad objectives into specific programs of behavior (intermediate supervisors). Large organizations may appear on paper as unitary structures, but in practice they are fragmented or, to use a term introduced earlier, disaggregated. Disaggregation, however, does not imply dissolution of organizations. In the next chapter we shall examine some of the mechanisms used to hold bureaucracies together when they become large and their structures dispersed.

3
The Two Authority Structures: Horizontal and Vertical Differentiation

The notion that bureaucratic structures vary is by now familiar to the reader. In this chapter we will introduce the idea that bureaucratic authority also varies, and that variations in authority patterns are linked to variations in structure. The dimensions of formal structure of most interest here are horizontal differentiation (the number of subunits in an organization) and vertical differentiation (the number of levels of hierarchy). Bureaucratic authority, however, is not as easily described as formal structure, largely because of the ambiguities and contradictions in theories of organizations, especially Weber's. We shall explore some of these before turning to specific hypotheses.

VARIATIONS IN AUTHORITY

The concept of bureaucratic authority has always been central to the analysis of formal organizations. Bureaucratic authority is distinguished from other types of authority because it is based on the office, not tradition or a person, and has its ultimate legitimacy in written laws and regulations rather than in customs or mores. Classical organization theory holds that bureaucratic authority provides the basis for coordination of the many dispersed parts of large organizations. Through numerous authority relationships, the goals of organizations are translated into directives for action and then transmitted through the hierarchy to the lower offices.

The most extensive discussion of authority, of course, is provided by Weber. Weber distinguished rational authority based on belief in the legality of rules and norms, and of the prerogatives of those in authority, from other types. But rational-legal authority, as Weber notes, is inextricably tied to the bureaucratic form of administration, hence the term *bureaucratic authority*.[1] The notion of bureaucratic authority like the idea of bureaucracy is to some extent an ideal-typical construct, because it is an abstract model with which many examples can be compared. One can say that authority relationships in a particular situation more or less fit the idea of rational-legal authority. The ideal-typical construct, however, does not allow for the different patterns of bureaucratic authority found in large organizations. Authority may be impersonal and legitimated by abstract standards, but at the same time it may be concentrated in one person in an organization or distributed among many. The rules of an organization may centralize authority in a few individuals, or authority may be centralized in the rules and regulations, which remove many decisions from the managerial hierarchy. Finally, Weber's notion of bureaucratic authority implies that the rules and regulations by which an organization operates are accessible and known to all its members, although they may not be. Differential access to the rules exists; there is variation in the extent to which members of organizations know the rules, and thus need not depend on their supervisors for direction.[2]

In this chapter we will argue that variations in bureaucratic authority patterns do indeed exist, and more importantly, that these variations are systematically related to the formal *structure* of bureaucratic organizations. The extent to which authroity to make decisions is centralized in the head of an organization rather than delegated among his subordinates, the extent to which regulations remove decisions from the managerial hierarchy, and the extent to which organizational regulations are known to all members are variable, and reflect fundamental differences in patterns of organization.[3] Authority rela-

---

[1] Weber's theory of bureaucratic authority is presented in *The Theory of Social and Economic Organizations*, trans. A. M. Henderson and Talcott Parsons (New York: Free Press, 1964), pp. 324-341.

[2] The concept of differential access to rules is discussed in Walter Miller, "Two Concepts of Authority," *American Anthropologist*, 57, 1955, 271-288.

[3] Again, our focus on organizational characteristics should be emphasized. Concepts, such as centralization of authority in bureaucratic regulations and accessibility of rules, are organizational, not individual, attributes.

tionships in bureaucratic organizations are not limited to the mono-cratic type which Weber's notions would have us believe. In effect, two seemingly disparate traditions in organizational research are linked here: the approach of Weber and some of the classical organization theorists to the study of organizational structure, which has paid little attention to the decision-making processes; and the approach to organizations which is largely concerned with the social psychology of decisions, and only tangentially with questions of formal structure.[4]

The idea that the formal structure of organizations is related to decision-making processes comes from several sources. The literature on business management offers several hypotheses, as does sociological research on bureaucracies, but these observations are by no means consistent. One hypothesis, for instance, is that as organizations become larger, and as the number of levels of hierarchy separating the head of the organization from nonsupervisory employees increases, efficiency requires most decision-making authority to be removed from top management and given to middle-level managers. In a multilevel structure, highly centralized decision-making authority would require an inordinate number of messages between top and bottom levels, overloading channels of communication.[5] Hence, from this perspective, multilevel hierarchies compel decentralization of control. But there is another literature which identifies multilevel structures with rigidity and centralization. Here it is said that one must have short and squat hierarchies in order to achieve decentralization.[6]

The continuing debate about separation of powers in government, which is reflected in some of the literature on public administration,

[4]See especially Herbert A. Simon, *Administrative Behavior,* 2d ed. (New York: Macmillan, 1957), and Daniel Katz and Robert L. Kahn, *The Social Psychology of Organizations* (New York: Wiley, 1966).

[5]There is a large literature on decentralization of authority in business organizations. One of the best accounts is Marshall E. Dimock, *Administrative Vitality* (New York: Harper & Row, 1959), chap. 13. For a sociological view of some dysfunctional consequences of centralized decision making in multilevel bureaucracies, see Michel Crozier, *The Bureaucratic Phenomenon* (Chicago: University of Chicago Press, 1964), part 1.

[6]See, for example, W. Lloyd Warner *et al., The Emergent American Society,* vol. 1, *Large Scale Organizations* (New Haven, Conn.: Yale University Press, 1967). Chapter 6, "The Changing Structure of a Great Corporation," describes the transition of General Electric Company from a centralized "vertical" hierarchy to a decentralized "flat" one.

also supports the notion that organizational structure affects authority practices. An implicit hypothesis is that as increasing numbers of subunits report directly to the head of a government bureau, there is a greater likelihood that requests for decisions and recommendations will be directed to him. thus centralizing control. This develops because the probability that any single decision will affect more than one subunit increases with their number, requiring the decision to be reviewed by their lowest common superior. Perhaps an illustration from Simon, Smithburg, and Thompson's work makes the point:

> Let us imagine a time when all the smallest work units of an organization handled all their own personnel functions. Then let us imagine that for one reason or another all personnel functions were removed from the units and a new personnel unit established in each section. In the former situation conflicts over personnel matters would be settled by the unit chief. . . . In the second situation (after a personnel unit had been established) conflicts over personnel matters would be settled by the section chief. . . . In this case we say that personnel functions have been centralized at the section level.[7]

The implication is that the greater the number of subunits or horizontal divisions of labor in an organization, the greater the extent to which authority is centralized in the head of the organization.[8] But, again, the opposite prediction is made. Some observers perceive a connection between relatively low ratios of subordinates to supervisors and overbearing bossism. Only by increasing the number of people who report to a manager, it is said, can abuses of hierarchical authority be curbed.[9]

Any structural change thus poses dilemmas. In the last chapter we noted that organizations differ from other types of groups because of the hierarchical arrangement of offices. Each member save for the boss reports to one and only one superior. Since supervisory spans of control

---

[9]Herbert A. Simon, Donald W. Smithburg, and Victor A. Thompson, *Public Administration* (New York: Knopf, 1956), pp. 272-273.
[8]"Horizontal" division of labor refers to the division of tasks among subunits, not individual persons in an organization.
[9]See, for example, James C. Worthy, "Organizational Structure and Employee Morale," *American Sociological Review*, 15, 1950, 169-179.

must be limited, increasing size compels greater differentiation; either added layers of hierarchy or new subunits are required. But neither of these expedients is without difficulties. By proliferating subunits a manager takes responsibility for coordination among them. He must devote much of his effort to this, which detracts from the time available for other matters, or an assistant can be hired to do the job, in which case a level of hierarchy is added. But as layers of hierarchy multiply, so do the number of intermediate positions between the boss and workers on the operating level. The cost of transmitting messages from top to bottom (or bottom to top) grows accordingly, while the likelihood of getting a message through without error diminishes. In other words, organizational hierarchies impose costs upon expansion because they require either vertical differentiation, horizontal differentiation, or both. The manager's task is to steer between the Scylla of overwork and the Charybdis of disorganization, but this is no easy task.

Bureaucratic structures are not easily changed, however, and administrative styles may be altered to fit the constraints of particular situations rather than the other way around. Where demand for decisions and managerial intervention is high, an autocratic style of administration will probably emerge. In part this reflects the need for speedy decisions, as careful consideration of all points of view is out of the question. But it also stimulates subordinates to behave according to the law of anticipated reactions:[10] Rather than bring issues to the boss, they attempt to resolve them as *he* would. Formal delegation of authority does not exist, but some matters are effectively kept from the boss. The presence of many subunits in an organization which increases demands made on top managers would thus seem to compel centralized operations. But where the boss's problem is securing adequate information, rather than being deluged by it, centralization becomes inappropriate. Delegation of authority is called for so long as decisions remain consistent and consonant with organizational purposes. The law of anticipated reactions does not work, however, because most employees are several levels removed from top managers and do not know what to anticipate; some other mechanism is needed to ensure consistency. Here it will be argued that authoritative rules and regulations and impersonal procedures for evaluating performance

[10]The rule of anticipated reactions is discussed by Simon, Smithburg, and Thompson, *Public Administration*, p. 196.

emerge in place of a direct means of control. Rules and regulations which are written and known to all do not depend on hierarchical channels of communication, and so become more useful as multilevel structures develop.[11]

If, by contrast, one wished to manipulate organizational structure to achieve centralized control, he would probably increase the number of direct links between the chief executive and lower-level personnel, shortening the lines of communication. This alters the table of organization in the same manner as the addition of several subunits, no matter what labels were attached to the newly created positions. Decentralization might be stimulated through the opposite process, by cutting lines of communication or rearranging offices so that there is more distance between executives and those who have first-hand knowledge of actual operations. Regardless of the direction of causality, then, multiunit organizational structures seem most compatible with centralized control while multilevel structures would seem to promote decentralization.

The hypotheses to be tested in this chapter may be summarized as follows:

1. Vertical differentiation, the proliferation of supervisory levels in an organization, is associated with decentralization of authority to make decisions.
2. Horizontal differentiation, the proliferation of subunits, is associated with centralization of decision-making authority.
3. Vertical differentiation is associated with formal rules and with rules that partly determine decisions in advance.

[11]Again, it should be noted that we are considering bureaucratic organizations, not collegial bodies whose members have internalized a set of professional norms or ethics. It should be noted, however, that the standards governing the behavior of professionals are always written and codified. See Harold Wilensky, "The Professionalization of Everyone," *American Journal of Sociology*, 70, 1964, 137-158. Wilensky points out that a formal code of ethics exists for all recognized professions.

A frequent source of tension in some organizations is conflict between bureaucratic standards and professional norms. Attorneys, accountants, and others who must hold dual loyalties—one to their employer, another to their profession—are often caught in this dilemma. Wilensky's *Intellectuals in Labor Unions* (New York: Free Press, 1956) is a classic study of this, but more recent accounts of this problem are remarkably scarce.

4. Horizontal differentiation is associated with the lack of formal rules, or with rules and practices that allow much discretion to top managers in making decisions.

The distinction between horizontal and vertical differentiation of bureaucracies resembles Duverger's idea of vertical and horizontal links in political organizations, but it is not the same thing. In Duverger's model vertical links connect superior and subordinate units, while horizontal links join units at the same level.[12] One might picture the organization chart of a vertically linked party organization as tall and narrow. By contrast, a horizontally linked organization may appear short and wide on a chart. The "shape" of a vertically linked party organization, then, resembles that of a vertically differentiated bureaucracy, and a horizontally linked party is like a horizontally differentiated organization. But there is a fundamental difference between Duverger's notions of linkage and the two modes of differentiation described here. Formally at least, no horizontal connections or lines of authority exist in bureaucracies. Though informal horizontal communication frequently occurs, vertical lines of authority are always preserved. In a political organization, by contrast, horizontal links are permitted to help maintain coordination of diverse units that lack a common superior. Since horizontal links do not exist in the formal organization of bureaucracies, one might speculate that the proliferation of supervisory levels (vertical differentiation) legitimates high rates of interaction among workers while preserving at the same time the fiction of a chain of command.

THE TWO STRUCTURES AND PATTERNS OF AUTHORITY

The hypotheses can be tested by examining the actual distribution of authority in finance departments. In the interviews, informants were asked, "What kinds of decision can division heads make without the approval of the head of the department? Can they make decisions about work assignments, budget allocations, or accounting procedures?" This question provides two indicators of delegation of authority to make decisions. Most informants told us about their

[12]Maurice Duverger, *Political Parties* (New York: Science Editions, Wiley, 1963), pp. 47-52.

practices in the three specific areas mentioned. About half said that division heads could decide about work assignments only, and half the informants said that division heads had, in addition, authority over budget allocations or accounting procedures, or both. Over 60 percent of the informants volunteered a statement of their policy in delegating authority to subordinates. The statements ranged from "I make all the decisions around here," to "My policy is to have decisions made on the lowest possible level." Table 4 shows the relationship of horizontal and vertical differentiation to division heads' authority to make specific kinds of decisions and department heads' policies in delegating authority.[13] Of the departments with few divisions when size is controlled (low horizontal differentiation), 50 percent permit division heads to decide about budget allocations or accounting procedures in addition to having authority over work assignments, compared with

---

[13]Horizontal differentiation is the residual difference between the actual number of divisions in a department and the number of divisions expected, given the regression equation relating the size of a department to the number of subunits in it. The residual number of divisions thus equals $Y_1 - .00723x - 5.027$, where Y_1 is the actual number of divisions in the department and x is the total number of employees in it. Horizontal differentiation is low when this expression is less than zero; it is high when the expression is positive. Low horizontal differentiation means that a department has fewer divisions than one would expect, given its size; high horizontal differentiation means that a department has more divisions than expected, given its size. The residuals are used in contingency tables because the high correlation of size and number of divisions render the usual multivariate analysis procedures unsuitable here. An ordinary two-variable table does not show the relationship of number of divisions to delegation of authority to make decisions, because the size of an organization will make the observed relationship spurious. But even if one controls for size and produces a three-way table in which the number of employees is held constant, the zero-order correlation between size and number of divisions indicates that *within the categories of size, departments with more divisions will have more employees.* Thus, the only way to control for size is to use residuals from a regression line. This involves the assumption that the underlying relationship between the number of employees and the number of divisions is linear. The distribution of the residuals shows that the regression is not altogether linear, but it seems better to make this assumption rather than to use a simpler method of analysis that severely limits possible findings. This discussion also applies to the measure of vertical differentiation.

Vertical differentiation is the residual difference between the actual number of levels in a department and the number of levels expected, given the regression equation relating the size of a department to the number of levels in it. The residual number of levels thus equals $Y_2 - .00272x - 3.649$, where Y_2 is the actual number of levels in the department and x is the total number of employees in it. Vertical differentiation is low when this expression is less than zero; it is high when the expression is positive.

41 percent in departments with high horizontal differentiation. (The difference is not statistically significant.) The same pattern appears in the policies of department heads toward delegating authority to their division chiefs. Table 4 shows that of the finance agencies with relatively few subunits, 61 percent give division heads responsibility for more than routine decisions, whereas in departments with many divisions, only 53 percent allow division heads such wide authority. (The difference is also not significant.) These data suggest, though hardly prove, that greater horizontal differentiation tends to centralize authority in the head of the department; increasing the number of subunits tends to channel decisions to the highest levels in organizations, thus removing authority from middle managers.

Vertical differentiation (the proliferation of supervisory levels) also affects the delegation of authority in bureaucratic organizations. Of departments with relatively few levels of net size, 43 percent allow division heads discretion to decide about budget allocations or accounting procedures, as compared with 50 percent in departments that have a relatively large number of supervisory levels. A stronger pattern emerges in the relation of vertical differentiation to department heads' policies about delegating authority. Table 4 shows that of the finance agencies with relatively few levels, 47 percent delegate most decisions to division heads, whereas among the departments with many supervisory levels, 71 percent delegate most decisions as a matter of policy. This difference is significant and consistent with the preceding data and with predictions. Horizontal differentiation tends to centralize decisions in the head of the department; by contrast, vertical differentiation is associated with delegation of decision-making authority to lower levels.

Informants were also asked who in the department *officially* recommends promotion or dismissal of employees when the occasion arises. Three-quarters of department heads reserve this power to themselves or their deputies, though in most cases informal advice from division heads is considered. Just as the distribution of authority to make decisions is affected by the formal structure of organizations, so is discretion over promotions and dismissals. As horizontal differentiation increases, the proportion of departments in which division heads have final authority in these matters drops from 29 to 21 percent. Vertical differentiation has the opposite effect; in departments with relatively few levels, 19

Table 4
Delegation of Authority to Make Decisions
by Horizontal and Vertical Differentiation

Delegation of Authority	Horizontal Differentiation		Vertical Differentiation	
	Low	High	Low	High
Decisions Delegated to Division Heads				
Work assignments only	50%	59%	57%	50%
Work assignments and other decisions	50	41	43	50
N	(115)	(93)	(115)	(93)
Department Head's Policy Is to Delegate				
Routine decisions	39%	47%	53%	29%
Most decisions	61	53	47	71
N	(87)	(72)	(90)	(69)
Promotion or Dismissal of Employees Is Officially Recommended by				
Department head or his deputy	71%	79%	81%	67%
Division heads	29	21	19	33
N	(136)	(106)	(137)	(105)

percent delegate decisions about advancements and firings to division heads while this proportion increases to 33 percent in multilevel departments. The two authority structures again have different consequences for centralization of authority in bureaucratic organizations.

Centralization of Authority in Bureaucratic Regulations

Bureaucratic regulations can centralize authority in the managerial hierarchy, or rules can remove decisions from the hierarchy so that the regulations themselves exert authority. A rule that concentrates authority in the managers might be one stating, "Decisions about promotion of employees are made solely by the head of the department." A rule that removes authority from the supervisory staff might state, by contrast, "Promotions are made on the basis of examination scores." Given a number of examination scores, this rule rather than any person decides who is to be promoted, so one can say that authority is centralized in the regulations. Informants were asked about the relative weights of examinations and personal evaluations in deciding about promotions. In the average department, examinations counted about one-third, and evaluations one-quarter. Other factors, of course, entered into the decision to promote an employee, such as seniority, education, and work experience, but these are not considered here.

It was predicted that among organizations with structures promoting decentralization of decisions, rules and regulations would themselves set criteria for decisions. In structures tending toward centralized decision making, one would expect few guidelines, since only a few people participate in decisions. Horizontal differentiation should be associated with increased importance of regulations that allow discretion to managers (evaluations) and decreased importance of rules that remove decisions from them (examinations). Table 5 shows that horizontal differentiation does have the expected effect on the importance of both evaluations and examinations. Of the departments with relatively few divisions, 54 percent attach substantial weight to evaluations, compared with 65 percent of departments of finance with many subunits. Horizontal differentiation thus increases the salience of rules that centralize authority to managers, and, as anticipated, it decreases the importance of rules that remove decisions from the managerial

Table 5
Importance of Evaluations and Examinations in Deciding
Promotions by Horizontal and Vertical Differentiation

	Horizontal Differentiation		Vertical Differentiation	
	Low	High	Low	High
Weight of Evaluations				
Less than 1/4	46%	35%	35%	49%
1/4 or more	54	65	65	51
N	(122)	(102)	(128)	(96)
Weight of Examinations				
Less than 1/3	43%	59%	56%	42%
1/3 or more	57	41	44	58
N	(122)	(102)	(128)	(96)

hierarchy. In departments with relatively few divisions, 57 percent place a high weight on examinations compared with 41 percent among departments with many divisions.

The expected pattern also emerges when the influence of vertical differentiation on the kinds of factors that enter into promotion decisions is considered. Table 5 shows that as relative number of supervisory levels increases, evaluations become less important, and examinations assume more weight in decisions about promotion. Of finance agencies with few levels of supervision, 65 percent attached great importance to evaluations in promotion decisions compared with 51 percent of multilevel departments. Just as vertical differentiation reduces the importance of rules that centralize authority in the managerial hierarchy, it increases the weight accorded examinations which remove decisions from the managers. Of the departments having relatively few levels, 44 percent count examinations less than one-third in promotion decisions, but 58 percent of the multilevel departments count examinations one-third or more. The data, then, confirm the general hypotheses. Horizontally differentiated bureaucracies emphasize the kinds of regulations that allow wide discretion to supervisors, and at the same time they attach relatively little importance to rules that set criteria for decisions and remove authority from the managers. By contrast, vertically differentiated bureaucracies give little weight to rules that centralize authority in the supervisory structure, and instead rely on regulations which to some extent determine decisions in advance. The two authority structures, then, have opposite implications for bureaucratic regulations. This is further evidence that the formal structure of a bureaucracy affects the exercise of authority in it.

Accessibility of the Rules

Accessibility to bureaucratic regulations limits to some extent the dependence of subordinates on top managers, and contributes to decentralization of authority. The presence of written rules governing promotions is used as an indicator of accessibility. It was predicted that rules are more accessible, that is, written and formalized, in vertically differentiated organizations than in those with relatively few levels, and less likely to be formalized in horizontally differentiated organizations than in others with few subunits. The second half of this hypothesis is not supported by the data. The same proportions of multiunit

Table 6
Use of Written Regulations in Deciding Promotions
by Vertical Differentiation

| | Vertical Differentiation | |
Written Regulations	Low	High
Yes	54%	69%
No	46	31
N	(139)	(113)

departments and those with relatively few divisions, 61 percent, have
written regulations that specify the criteria for promotions. Perhaps this
reflects a reluctance of department heads to withdraw rules once they
have been written, even though the other data indicate that authority
does accrue to top managers as the number of subunits increases.
Accessibility to the rules does, however, increase with the number of
hierarchical levels in an organization. Table 6 shows that, of departments with relatively few levels, 54 percent are bound by written
regulations in promotion decisions, compared with 69 percent of
vertically differentiated departments. The proliferation of supervisory
levels, then, tends to increase the probability that regulations are
written and thus accessible to members of an organization. The more
accessible the rules are, the less supervisors can claim exclusive
knowledge of them, and so the greater the extent to which authority is
removed from the hierarchical structure and vested instead in the
regulations. Rules may be formalized primarily to remove ambiguity
and ensure their uniform application, but the latent function of written
regulations is to distribute authority throughout a bureaucracy rather
than leave it centralized in one person.

CENTRALIZED VERSUS DISPERSED AUTHORITY

The authority structures of finance departments have been described by
two variables, horizontal differentiation and vertical differentiation, the
proliferation of subunits and supervisory levels, respectively. These two
variables generally have opposite consequences for other variables
describing authority relationships in bureaucracies. Vertical differentia-

tion increases the delegation of decisions to lower levels in organizations; horizontal differentiation increases the centralization of decision-making authority in the head of the department. Vertical differentiation increases the importance of rules that remove decisions from the managerial hierarchy; horizontal differentiation increases the importance of rules and practices that allow authority to accrue to top managers. Finally, vertical differentiation increases the extent to which the rules are accessible to all members of an organization.

These findings indicate that formal structures of authority influence actual authority practices. Horizontal differentiation is concomitant with what one might call *centralized* authority. Centralized authority makes the top manager or managers important in the ordinary operations of a bureaucracy. Not only does management make policy, but it also translates the generalities of policy into the specifics of commands, very much blurring the distinction between the two. An organization thus becomes increasingly sensitive to the directions of the head, and much communication flows to and from him. Centralized authority, then, renders a bureaucracy very responsive to the wishes of managers and very flexible in its operations. But centralized authority in an organization may also make its operations very erratic, preventing consistent operations which are critical, according to Weber's model of bureaucracy.

By contrast, vertical differentiation in organizations is concomitant with *dispersed* authority, where lower-level managers make decisions according to principles elaborated by their superiors. Where dispersed authority prevails, a clear separation exists between those who decide on goals and those who translate them into commands for action. Fewer messages are transmitted through the hierarchy than where centralized authority prevails; the organization relies on competent specialists to translate general policies into specific instructions for subordinates. This pattern of authority is directed toward technical perfection in the operations of a bureaucracy. It can be very cumbersome, but it is also a very effective form of administration in that its operations remain constant from day to day and do not depend on the person who heads the organization.

These conjectures are partly supported by some recent experimental evidence. Carzo and Yanouzas designed two types of organizations with fifteen members each. One, the flat structure, had a president and fourteen subordinate members who reported directly to him. The other, the tall structure, had four levels with spans of control of two throughout. Each organization was assigned the task of deciding the probable demand for its products and the optimal allocation of goods to the various geographical areas for which subordinate members were responsible. Profitability and rates of return on investment were computed after each decision, and subjects were rewarded accordingly.[14]

Several strong findings emerged from the research. The one most pertinent to this discussion is that decisions took no longer in tall structures than in flat ones. Short lines of communication in flat structures presumably speed decisions, but this benefit is more than offset by the debate and conflict that developed when one boss had to allocate scarce resources among fourteen subordinates. In the tall structure, Carzo and Yanouzas note, "Discussions were more orderly and resolution was faster because the president and intermediate supervisors had to deal with only two subordinates."[15] In addition, organizations with tall structures were more profitable and had higher rates of return than the flat structures; the investigators surmised that narrow spans of control allowed for more intensive analysis and repeated evaluation of decisions which contributed to effective performance.[16]

A critical variable, differences in status, was omitted from the experiment. Supervisors neither evaluated nor rewarded subordinates. We cannot be sure whether the speed of decisions would have changed had the experimental groups more nearly resembled actual organizations. Nor do we know what criteria would have emerged for evaluating members of the different organizations. But despite the limitations of the experiment, a relationship between wide spans of control of executives, conflict among their immediate subordinates, and centralization of decisions were indicated. Flat structures, those which were

[14]Rocco Carzo, Jr., and John N. Yanouzas, "Effects of Flat and Tall Organization Structure," *Administrative Science Quarterly,* 14, 1969, 178-191.
[15]*Ibid.,* 189.
[16]Again, the variable of technology rears its ugly head. Implicit in this discussion is the hypothesis that economies of scale decline with increasing technical interdependencies in organizations. Had we studied a set of diverse organizations (i.e., chain gangs, bureaus, and surgical teams) we might have been able to test this notion, but the present research is confined to bureaucratic organizations for reasons already explained.

horizontally differentiated, generated erratic and ineffective decision making, while the opposite held for tall, vertically differentiated structures.

AUTHORITY AND RATIONALITY

Despite the intention to avoid testing Weber's notions of bureaucracy, a question is inevitably raised about possible inconsistencies in his ideal-typical construct. Other observers, notably Udy and Stinchcombe, have found that not all "rational" organizations fit the bureaucratic model. Their separate studies of very different organizations indicate that some "bureaucratic" attributes, elaborate hierarchies of authority and sizable administrative staffs, do not necessarily emerge alongside certain "rational" attributes, specialization and rewards based on performance.[17] The present findings show that elongated hierarchies and rules which remove authority from managers are not conducive to centralized decision making which, according to Weber, epitomizes bureaucracy. One more amendment to Weber's model is thus suggested.

The more important question concerns the impact of organizational arrangements on what is rational for individual persons. The two authority structures that have been described use different mechanisms to elicit more or less predictable behavior from people. One, the centralized organization, operates through direct orders and face-to-face authority; little discretion is allowed. The other, dispersed authority, permits many people to make decisions but insists that they do so according to rules and regulations.

Although it is possible that people's behavior is equally constrained in the two structures, it is not similarly constrained. Centralized authority makes it rational to follow managerial directives and little else. The use of "one's own insights into the interrelations of events" (as Mannheim defines substantial rationality) is neither necessary nor rewarded. Dispersed authority demands a very different sort of rationality: One must reconcile various alternatives with the decision premises provided

[17]Arthur L. Stinchcombe, "Bureaucratic and Craft Administration of Production," *Administrative Science Quarterly,* 4, 1959, 168-187; Stanley H. Udy, Jr., " 'Bureaucracy' and 'Rationality' in Weber's Theory," *American Sociological Review,* 24, 1959, 791-795.

by rules and regulations.[18] If the rules anticipated all possible situations, this process could be as automatic as following the boss's orders.[19] But, in fact, there are usually ambiguities and inconsistencies in rules which require the use of judgment. More important, rules and regulations affect managers as well as their subordinates. A supervisor's request that is inconsistent with the rules, or beyond their scope, can be rejected by a subordinate, whereas he would be vulnerable to any request without protection of the rules. At least the possibility for substantial rationality exists under these circumstances.

Inevitably, a question is raised about the causes of horizontal and vertical differentiation in bureaucracies. The data allow no clear answer to this, but they do offer some suggestive evidence. Vertical differentiation, we may surmise, reflects fundamental administrative considerations in organizations. If for no other reason, organizations seek to limit ratios of subordinates to supervisors so managers can actually manage. And, as we saw in the last chapter, proliferation of vertical levels may reflect deliberate efforts to separate nonoperational from operational objectives, policy from implementation. The causes of horizontal differentiation, particularly at higher levels of bureaucracies, are not easily identified. A few of the finance departments studied have as many as twenty divisions or bureaus reporting to the department head, more than reasonable or prudent for any executive. One tentative explanation is provided by James D. Thompson, who notes that organizations in heterogeneous task environments tend to establish separate structural units to deal with each part of the environment.[20] This would suggest that horizontal differentiation is most intense in those finance departments which view their environments as heterogeneous and uncontrollable. By contrast departments which have successfully reduced heterogeneous environments to a manageable

---

[18]Decision premises are discussed in the introduction to Simon, *Administrative Behavior.*

[19]Popular stereotypes of bureaucracy find rules and regulations inflexible and a source of irritation to clients. How public bureaucracies might operate in the absence of formalized procedures is rarely considered, and it ought to be. Officials of public agencies have a great deal of power over clients: They can grant or withhold resources not obtainable elsewhere. In the absence of elaborate codes, clients would be subject to the whims of bureaucrats and, what is worse, lack means of appealing adverse decisions.

[20]James D. Thompson, *Organizations in Action* (New York: McGraw-Hill, 1967), p. 70.

number of homogenous segments are less likely to proliferate units, but rather attend to common sense administrative considerations such as keeping spans of control within bounds. One can easily imagine that much more discretion, indeed power, accrues to employees in agencies that have control over their environments than in organizations that lack control.

The findings from the previous chapter and this one suggest a fundamental dynamic to organizations which is reflected in people's behavior as members of them. There is the constant tension between "holding on" and "letting go," between maintaining centralized control where few people determine virtually everything that takes place in an organization and dispersing authority so that wide participation in decisions is attained, but only after mechanisms to ensure consistency and coordination of activities have been devised. The smallest organizations are so much like informal groups that this is no problem, but as they grow there is an initial tendency toward centralization of decisions. But at the same time, growth compels separation of nonoperational from operational goals, and intermediate managerial levels emerge to link the two. This, in turn, is conducive to decentralization, if only because of the high cost of communication from top to bottom in multilevel structures. But decentralization cannot take place unless procedures exist to guide decisions and guarantee fairness; hence written rules and impersonal mechanisms of control such as examinations are developed. Once established, however, rules and impersonal mechanisms are recognized as authoritative, and tend to limit people's discretion.[21] An equilibrium of sorts between forces that would centralize and forces that would disperse organizations is thus maintained.

When one speaks of an equilibrium in organizations or anywhere else, simple cause and effect notions are usually absent. Rather, one assumes interdependent relationships among a set of variables which operate to preserve stability or order in the system. Just what remains stable or ordered is usually not specified. The present discussion, by contrast, attempts to integrate ideas about cause and effect with equilibrium notions. In particular, we have identified changes in size and structural

[21]Robert K. Merton's classic article uses the term "displacement of goals" to describe overconformity to bureaucratic regulations. See "Bureaucratic Structure and Personality," in *Social Theory and Social Structure,* 2d ed. rev. (New York: Free Press, 1957), pp. 195-209.

differentiation as the sources of changes in mechanisms organizations use to preserve control and coordination. An explicit assumption is that control and coordination are present to some degree in all viable organizations. Given this assumption, the data suggest a balance between centralizing and decentralizing or disorganizing tendencies in bureaucracies; the more of one, the more of the other. Increased size or differentiation may alter the balance, but in the long run, organizational effectiveness is impaired unless restorative mechanisms are introduced.

Though variations in size and structural differentiation are associated with different means of maintaining order, they are not the only characteristics of organizations which affect authority practices. We have yet to consider the implications of advanced technologies or of how an organization's tasks are divided among its subunits on coordination and control in bureaucracies. The next two chapters will pursue these topics.

4
The Impact
of Automation

"THEORY X" AND "THEORY Y"

Most theories of organizations can be conveniently reduced to either "Theory X" or "Theory Y." The former, "Theory X," stresses formal organization, authority, and administrative process; "Theory Y" emphasizes motivation, human relations, and informal processes in work organizations. The divergent approaches to organizational theory force proponents of either side to put their arguments into perspective. Advocates of "Theory X" must continually acknowledge that human relations *do* make a difference; similarly, human relations specialists from time to time concede that formal properties of organizations have some impact on the kinds of behavior they study.

Empirical research on organizations has not been so neatly balanced as the theories. The great majority of researchers have dealt with "Theory Y," the problems of human relations in organizations. The work of Roethlisberger and Dickson, of Whyte, of Katz and Kahn,[1] and of many others is largely concerned with individual behavior in an organizational setting. The problems of organization, or formal organization as it is so often called, are usually relegated to sociologists or students of public administration rather than treated by organizational specialists. The sociologists have examined the relationship between "formal" and

[1] Fritz J. Roethlisberger and William J. Dickson, *Management and the Worker* (Cambridge, Mass.: Harvard University Press, 1939); William F. Whyte, *Human Relations in the Restaurant Industry* (New York: McGraw-Hill, 1948); Daniel Katz and Robert L. Kahn, *The Social Psychology of Organizations* (New York: Wiley, 1964).

"informal" organization;[2] political scientists interested in administration have elaborated numerous theories, but few empirical findings, to confirm or disconfirm them.[3] That empirical knowledge of organizations consists for the most part of propositions about human relations is hardly surprising. There exist numerous psychological and social-psychological propositions that have been tested in the laboratory and that seem readily applicable to behavior in organizations. By contrast, there exists no comparable body of knowledge about organizations per se.

The study of the impact of automation in organizations perhaps best illustrates this disparity between theories and empirical research. Automation, *as an organizational phenomenon,* is extremely important because of the way it can change fundamental administrative processes. Yet there have been few studies of organizational changes associated with the use of computers. Instead, researchers have for the most part concentrated on the effects of automation on the behavior and feelings of the individual worker. And as is so often the case in the social sciences, only contradictory findings have emerged. It is found, for instance, that automation decreases workers' satisfaction with their jobs, almost to the point of quitting.[4] Ironically, the same study reports that in the long run workers derive satisfaction and pride from the same factors that earlier caused discontent. It has been argued that automation reduces the need for supervision and allows wider participation in decision making, but some empirical results have shown just the opposite.[5] Finally, a number of commentators have predicted that automation will help upgrade jobs and cause the replacement of the working class by what Daniel Bell terms a white-collar *salariat.*[6] But again there is contradictory evidence. At least one study shows that

[2]Peter M. Blau, *The Dynamics of Bureaucracy,* 2d ed. rev. (Chicago: University of Chicago Press, 1963); Alvin W. Gouldner, *Patterns of Industrial Bureaucracy* (New York: Free Press, 1954).
[3]Herbert A. Simon, *Administrative Behavior* (New York: Macmillan, 1957); Dwight Waldo, *The Administrative State* (New York: Ronald, 1948).
[4]Charles R. Walker, *Toward the Automatic Factory* (New Haven, Conn.: Yale University Press, 1957).
[5]Floyd L. Mann and Lawrence K. Williams, "Observations on the Dynamics of a Change to Electronic Data-Processing Equipment," *Administrative Science Quarterly,* 5, 1960, 217-256; Thomas L. Whisler and George P. Schultz, "Automation and the Management Process," *Annals,* 340, March, 1962, 81-89.
[6]Daniel Bell, "Work and Its Discontents," in *The End of Ideology* (New York: Free Press, 1960), pp. 222-262.

automation reduces the level of required skill and increases the tedium of a worker's job.[7]

The studies of the effect of automation on human relations are not to be criticized because of their inconsistent findings; that is almost inevitable. They are to be criticized, instead, because they study the wrong thing. There is an implicit assumption in human relations research on automation that has never been substantiated. The assumption is roughly this: The impact of automation on the worker is direct; it is not mediated by formal organizational structure (for example, the hierarchy of authority, division of labor, rules, regulations). This assumption is rejected here. The effects of automation on human relations should be assessed only after taking into account the changes in organizational processes which automation itself engenders. This chapter will show that the use of a computer changes the administrative structure of organizations. Having shown this, it will then discuss implications for both classical organizational theory and human relations theory.

THE DATA-PROCESSING STAFF
AND THE PROBLEM OF INTERDEPENDENCE

Automation, the use of computers, as a technical innovation probably has little impact on formal bureaucratic structure, but how the data-processing function is organized in a bureaucracy does have important effects on administrative processes. Two factors should be noted. First, most automated organizations have a separate data-processing staff. Of the finance departments in this study, 86 percent of those which use a computer have a data-processing staff. This staff is unique because its members are specialists in the operations of the computer, and so have skills which other members of the organization do not understand. A second factor is that the data-processing activity is not itself a primary goal of organizations. Rather, it is intended only as an efficient means to organizational goals. Were computers inefficient, they would not be used. Perhaps this last point belabors the obvious, but it leads to the following formulation: The data-processing

[7]James R. Bright, "Does Automation Raise Skill Requirements?" *Harvard Business Review,* 36, no. 4, July-August, 1958, 85-89.

staff, composed of specialists whose work is not understood by others, performs a service for other units of an organization by quickly and cheaply doing tasks that would otherwise occupy many employees.

The formation of a data-processing staff, then, creates interdependence in an organization. The various line units, those whose activities contribute directly to organizational goals, must rely on the performance of the data-processing staff to accomplish their goals. A great deal of communication between line units and the data-processing staff is thus required so that their efforts can be coordinated. If such communication is absent or breaks down, then the data-processing staff cannot make its contribution, and automation will seem to have failed. Communication between line units and the data-processing staff can be maintained in several ways. One could, if he wished, insist that all messages go vertically "through channels." Thus, a message between members of line and data-processing units would be transmitted upward through the hierarchy until it reached their lowest common superior (that is, the person lowest in the hierarchy who has jurisdiction over both), and then sent downward to its recipient.[8] This, however, is likely to be a very expensive way of achieving coordination. The hierarchical channels would become so overburdened with messages that an inordinate proportion of an organization's effort would be devoted to maintaining communication between line units and the data-processing staff. Whatever efficiencies resulted from automation would be more than lost in this attempt to preserve hierarchical coordination in an organization characterized by interdependent subunits.

In practice, of course, most organizations tacitly permit or even encourage horizontal (that is, nonhierarchical) communication among members. Even where it is illicit, horizontal communication frequently takes place in bureaucracies.[9] Where it is neither prohibited nor allowed for in a table of organization, horizontal communication sometimes results in better coordination of an organization's activities than might occur if supervisors intervened in the situation.[10] Most organizations simply allow horizontal communications to take place because it poses

[8]This practice of excessive "hierarchicalism" was quite common in pre-World War II French bureaucracy. See Walter R. Sharp, *The French Civil Service: Bureaucracy in Transition* (New York: Macmillan, 1931), pp. 40-42.
[9]See Blau, *Dynamics of Bureaucracy,* chap. 7.
[10]See Richard L. Simpson, "Vertical and Horizontal Communication in Formal Organizations," *Administrative Science Quarterly,* 4, 1959, 188-196.

no real problems in day-to-day operations. Among peers (employees of roughly equal status), horizontal interchanges and cooperative relationships rarely cause trouble, especially if the precepts of human relations theory are followed. Among employees who hold very different statuses in an organization, deference (*not* authority, which presumably operates only in hierarchical situations) permits cooperation of sorts to emerge in nonhierarchical relationships.

The problem of interdependence and horizontal communication, however, is not solved by indirection when it is caused by the presence of a data-processing staff in an organization. The "clients" of a data-processing staff are most frequently heads of line units or their assistants; nonsupervisory line personnel have little to do with data processing. The head of a line division is of high status in the organization, but he probably understands little about what the computer (and the data-processing staff) can and cannot do for him. In this sense, he is of low expertness. If the situation goes unchecked, it is likely that he will have to deal with a member of the data-processing staff who occupies a fairly low status in the organization, a programmer or systems analyst who has no supervisory responsibility but who is of high expertness because of his knowledge of the computer. Cooperative relationships are very difficult to maintain under these circumstances. The line manger may, because of his low expertness, make unreasonable requests of the data-processing staff. What is worse, he may attempt to insist that these requests be fulfilled by asserting the authority of his office.

The data-processing specialist may, in return, deny an unreasonable request (or sometimes a reasonable one if it is inconvenient) by asserting the authority of his expertness. He, not his high-status client, understands the intricacies of the computer. Disagreements, noncooperation, and avoidance behavior thus characterize relationships between superior nonexperts and subordinate experts; this is often called *line-staff conflict.*[11]

---

[11]Victor A. Thompson has discussed at length the problem of relationships between nonexpert superiors and expert subordinates. See "Hierarchy, Specialization, and Organizational Conflict," *Administrative Science Quarterly,* 5, 1961, 511-512. See also Thompson's *Modern Organization* (New York: Knopf, 1951), where he labels the dysfunctional aspects of expert-nonexpert relationships as "bureaupathic" behavior. Jack Seigman and Bernard Karsh in "Some Organizational Correlates of White Collar Automation," *Sociological Inquiry,* 32, 108-116, describe a case of organizational conflict resulting from the use of a computer.

One could interpret the difficult relationship between line managers and data-processing specialists as a human relations problem, but in this chapter it will be considered as a result of a type of bureaucratic structure that compels high-status nonexperts and low-status experts to cooperate with one another. In other words, the tensions and strains so often associated with automation are in part caused by administrative arrangements that become inadequate as interdependence increases in an organization. We hypothesize here that many organizations, when faced with the problem of interdependence between dispersed parts, adapt to this situation by altering their formal structure. In particular, the role of the consultant, a high-status member of the data-processing staff who is primarily responsible for coordinating the work of line units with that of computer specialists, is institutionalized as interdependence increases.

The consultant is a member of the data-processing staff who at least nominally holds a high-level supervisory position. He spends little of his time supervising, however, because he is primarily concerned with the task of coordination. From the perspective of classical organizational theory, the consultant's role is an anomaly; he is a supervisor whose job is not to supervise. But as a matter of organizational practice, the consultant's role is a useful innovation. Because the consultant is of high status, a line manager cannot dominate him by asserting the authority of his office. For the same reason, line managers have little reason to suspect the consultant of using his expertness to augment his power in the organization. Thus, in developing the consultant's role, some of the difficulties inherent in the line-staff relationships may be avoided. The data-processing staff, then, is distinguished from other parts of an organization by its hierarchy of authority which includes one or more consultants, members who have supervisory authority but whose real task is to maintain coordination between line units and data-processing specialists.

Before turning to the data, perhaps it would be best to outline the model suggested above:

1. In automated organizations, a staff of data-processing specialists whose work is not understood by others runs the computer.
2. Data processing is not an organizational goal, but only a means to a goal; thus, there is much interdependence between the data-processing staff and the line units.

3. Interdependence requires horizontal communications between an organization's units, but if no changes are made in traditional forms of organization, high-status members of line units must deal with low-status data-processing experts.
4. Cooperation between high-status nonexperts and low-status experts is difficult to maintain and is a source of much tension. Thus, many organizations evolve the consultant's role so that high-status members of line divisions deal only with a high-status member of the data-processing unit.

ANALYZING DIFFERENCES WITHIN ORGANIZATIONS

Here, as in part of the next chapter, differences between divisions as well as between departments will be analyzed. In considering data that describe divisions, we shall compare the unit which has primary responsibility for the data-processing activity to the other units of an organization. To do this, a three-way classification of departments and divisions is used; it appears in Table 7. The first column presents data for the 121 departments in which there is no data-processing division. Among these departments, for example, there is an average of 2.84 levels of supervision (including the nonsupervisory level) *in each division,* and the mean number of employees for whom each first-line supervisor is responsible is 6.62. The data in the center column describe departments which have a data-processing division, but the division in charge of the computer has been excluded from the calculation of means. Thus, excluding the data-processing units, automated departments have an average of 2.97 levels of supervision in divisions, and the span of control of first-line supervisors is 7.22. The final column includes only data-processing divisions. These divisions have a mean of 3.28 levels of supervision, and the average span of control over nonsupervisory employees is 8.55.

Perhaps we should first consider how the presence of a data-processing unit affects an organization's use of highly qualified personnel. One might think that data-processing experts are more likely to have college degrees than other employees in finance departments. The bottom row of Table 7 shows that this is not the case, however. Divisions in charge of data processing have a lower proportion of positions for which a college degree is desired (19.5 percent) than divisions of nonautomated

Table 7
Structural Differentiation and Supervisory Practices by Automation in Departments and Divisions (Means and Standard Errors)

Variable	Nonautomated Departments, Average of All Divisions	Automated Departments	
		Average of Line Division	Data-Processing Division
Levels of Hierarchy	2.84	2.97	3.28
Error	0.08	0.05	0.06
Span of Control of First-Line Supervisors	6.62	7.22	8.55
Error	0.44	0.28	0.34
Span of Control of Intermediate Supervisors	1.58	1.57	1.27
Error	0.10	0.07	0.04
Proportion of Time First-Line Supervisors Supervise	0.367	0.331	0.414
Error	0.019	0.014	0.013
Proportion of Time Intermediate Supervisors Supervise	0.417	0.435	0.385
Error	0.025	0.017	0.013
Proportion of Employees for Whom a College Degree Is Desired	0.259	0.299	0.195
Error	0.017	0.014	0.006
Number of Departments	121	133	

departments (25.9 percent) or line divisions of automated departments (29.9 percent). Although a data-processing unit employs many workers who lack high educational qualifications, the use of a computer increases the need for highly qualified personnel in other parts of an organization. Some small part of the difference between data-processing sections and other units in automated departments may result from the transfer of workers with low qualifications from other units to the section in charge of the computer. But most of the difference reflects a genuine need for more highly qualified personnel. The operation and maintenance of a computer do not require the generalized competence that a college education provides, but planning for the use of a computer and evaluation of the results which take place in line divisions do require a high level of competence. The uneven distribution of college-trained personnel between the data-processing staff and the line divisions of an organization probably exacerbates the difficulties caused by interdependence. Relations between high-status line managers and low-status computer experts become all the more strained because of the disparity between the educational qualifications of these groups. The manager who possesses a college degree probably would find it quite trying to cooperate with, and depend upon, a data-processing specialist who, compared with the manager, is uneducated. Thus, development of the coordinator's role becomes all the more important in automated organizations.

Table 7 also shows that the formal structure, the distribution of offices, in data-processing divisions differs from that in other subunits of finance departments. Data-processing divisions have more levels of hierarchy (3.28) than other divisions of automated departments (2.97) or divisions in nonautomated departments (2.84). The average span of control of first-line supervisors is also higher in data-processing divisions (8.55) than in either other sections of automated finance agencies (7.22) or departments that have no data-processing unit (6.62). Finally, higher supervisors are responsible for fewer employees in computer sections (1.27) than in other subunits of automated departments (1.57) or in nonautomated departments (1.58). These differences between data-processing divisions and other subunits are statistically significant. It should also be noted that these findings are not artifacts of the numbers of employees in divisions. Data-processing divisions are slightly larger than others, but the differences in size are not significant.

Let us summarize the present findings by constructing models of divisions which the data suggest. The models in Figure 4 exaggerate the differences we have found, but they show the distinctive features of a data-processing division when compared with other divisions. In the models, there are four levels in the data-processing unit and three in the other division. The span of control of the first-line supervisors is eight and that of higher supervisors is one in the data-processing division; the first-line span of control is four and the higher-level span of control two in the hypothetical other division. The models show that the differences between data-processing and other divisions which we have observed can be explained as the result of change in the position of one or two supervisors. The position of a first-line supervisor is moved so that other first-line supervisors report to him and he, in turn, reports to the division head. This change increases simultaneously the number of hierarchical levels, increases the average span of control of first-line

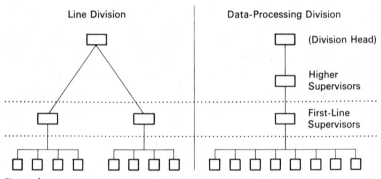

Figure 4:
Two Models of Divisions

supervisors, and decreases the span of control of higher supervisors. Data-processing sections, then, assume a more vertically differentiated structure than other subunits of a finance department. The number of supervisory levels, importantly, is increased by differentiating among supervisory personnel rather than by assigning supervisory positions to formerly nonsupervisory personnel.

The unique structure of a data-processing section partly reflects the amount of planning and coordination that must take place within the unit so that it can service other parts of the department. Higher managers in the data-processing division spend less of their time (38.5 percent of it) supervising than do higher managers in other divisions of automated departments (43.5 percent) or their counterparts in non-automated agencies (41.7 percent, though this difference is not significant). The work of higher supervisors in data-processing units involves relatively little supervision and, we suspect, much advising and consultation with members of other divisions to cope with the problems inherent in the use of a computer. A seeming paradox of automation is that it creates an extra level of supervisors whose job is not to supervise. But this paradox helps to resolve potential line-staff conflict. By having high-status managers who act as consultants to others over whom they do not have formal jurisdiction, one avoids situations in which low-status staff specialists attempt to give authoritative advice to high-status nonexperts.

The special structure of data-processing units is also reflected in the activities of first-line supervisors. The managers who direct the work of nonsupervisory personnel in the data-processing division spend more of their time supervising (41.4 percent) than other first-line supervisors in automated departments (33.1 percent) or first-line managers in non-automated departments (36.7 percent, though again this difference is not significant). These differences can be attributed, to some extent, to the wide spans of control that first-line supervisors have in data-processing divisions. These differences also create discontinuities in the authority structure of data-processing units. Such discontinuities occur when an intermediate level of managers has less supervisory responsibility than first-line managers. From Table 7, it is clear that in both nonautomated departments and line divisions of automated ones, higher managers spend more of their time supervising than do first-line supervisors. The higher one ascends the hierarchy, the more supervisory responsibility he has. This is not the case among data-processing divisions, where, if anything, the opposite takes place; first-line managers spend more time supervising than do their superiors. Perhaps one latent function of such hierarchical discontinuities is to render lower-level data-processing personnel "unavailable" to top managers.[12]

---

[12]We use the word "unavailable" to connote insulation of lower-level personnel from the direct demands of top managers. This meaning is taken from Kornhauser's use of "available" in a political context: the ability of elites to mobilize nonelites. See William Kornhauser, *The Politics of Mass Society* (New York: Free Press, 1959).

The proliferation of supervisory levels and discontinuities in the authority structure make it unlikely that high-status but nonspecialist managers can make requests directly of low-status data-processing specialists, thus averting another source of line-staff conflict.

IMPLICATIONS FOR THEORIES OF ORGANIZATIONS

The present findings necessitate some comment on both the classical and human relations theories of organizations. Most theories of organizational structure hold in common the notion that the use of hierarchical authority ought to be the principal means by which the activities of dispersed parts of organizations are coordinated. Weber speaks of "strict super- and subordination" that characterizes bureaucracies. Gulick and Urwick, attempting to salvage the notion that all relationships within bureaucratic structures are hierarchical ones, devise the administrative fiction that the staff acts in the name of the head of the organization and that for this reason, not its expertness, the advice of staff members ought to be followed. Even March and Simon make no allowance for interdependence and nonhierarchical forms of coordination in this process. Only James D. Thompson has explicitly considered this problem, but his central point is that rationality requires interdependence to be confined to relatively small units.[13] The findings here indicate that theories of formal organization ought to pay more attention to interdependence and its implications for administrative practice. A simple proposition is advanced as a contribution to theories of formal organizational structure: As interdependence in an organization increases, nonhierarchical forms of cooperation and the coordinator's role tend to emerge.

The coordinator's role effectively reduces the importance of formal hierarchical positions and allows for exercise of discretion in a manner not anticipated by traditional theories of bureaucracy. It does so largely because the rate of technological change in organizations has increased beyond the ability of managers to be more knowledgeable than subordinate specialists. This creates potential for conflict, but it also

[13]Max Weber, "Bureaucracy," in *From Max Weber: Essays in Sociology,* eds. H. Gerth and C. W. Mills (New York: Oxford University Press, 1946), pp. 196-244; Luther Gulick and L. Urwick, *Papers in the Science of Administration* (New York: Institute of Public Administration, 1937); James G. March and Herbert A. Simon, *Organizations* (New York: Wiley, 1958), chap. 6; James D. Thompson, *Organizations in Action* (New York: McGraw-Hill, 1967), chap. 5.

compels executives to "let go" and permit others over whom they nominally hold authority, not just formally designated subordinates, to make decisions affecting the whole organization. In this sense, technological innovations such as automation create possibilities for individual autonomy by reducing subordinates' dependence on a boss who determines what ends can be pursued.

It has been argued elsewhere that this process is only a transitory one. Once top managers master the intricacies of the computer, it is claimed, there will be recentralization of control and further erosion of workers' ability to make meaningful judgments, and even of their privacy.[14] There is considerable evidence that automation reduces the cost of information and the time and manpower needed to make decisions,[15] but whether this will lead to concentration of control or to more frequent and thorough decisions is a moot question. In all likelihood, some organizations will use the computer to buttress the line of authority, but if experience to date is meaningful, those with the most traditional managerial practices will be most resistant to automation.[16] More important, the present pace of technological change will probably continue. Today's experts who will become tomorrow's managers may soon have to deal with subordinates whose work they too do not understand.

From the perspective of human relations theory it is very important whether or not an organization retains a traditional vertical structure as interdependence increases. If a data-processing unit is superimposed on an older organizational form without other adjustments, then human relations are likely to suffer. Difficulties and delays in communication between line units and the data-processing staff are one source of frustration. Another problem is line-staff conflict which was discussed earlier: Who has final authority when differences arise between the

[14]See Harold J. Leavitt and Thomas L. Whisler, "Management in the 1980's," *Harvard Business Review*, 36, no. 6, 1958, 41-48.

[15]One of the best illustrations of economies afforded by automation is Michael S. Scott-Morton's research on production scheduling. See "Computer-Driven Visual Display Devices: Their Impact on the Management Decision-Making Process," unpublished D.B.A. thesis, Harvard Graduate School of Business Administration (Boston, 1967).

[16]This problem is discussed in Michel Crozier, *The Bureaucratic Phenomenon* (Chicago: University of Chicago Press, 1964), chap. 10. Arthur L. Stinchcombe also argues that an organization's age is an important determinant of its structure. See "Social Structure and Organizations," in *Handbook of Organizations*, ed. James G. March (Chicago: Rand McNally, 1966), pp. 142-193.

computer experts and line managers? In traditional line organizations which allow only vertical channels of communications, these differences will all too frequently have to be resolved by the head of the organization, overburdening him with demands for decisions. Ultimately, this leads to high centralization of control, which in itself tends to contribute to an authoritarian atmosphere and poor human relations. If, by contrast, an organization can dispense with the concept of a rigid chain of command and allow horizontal interchange, then automation will have little impact on its members' ability to cooperate with one another.

More generally, a point made in the initial discussion should be restated here. One cannot assume that there is a simple relationship between the use of a computer in an organization and its impact on human relations among employees. Organizational structure—the arrangement of work by divisions or subunits and by levels of hierarchy, and the channels of communication that are available to employees—intervenes between automation and its effects on workers. Older organizations and those which maintain the most rigid hierarchical arrangements will probably experience the greatest difficulties with automation. Thus organizational structure, not the use of a computer in and of itself, may be the proximate cause of the human relations problems so often associated with automation.

5
Interdependence versus Self-containment

THE THEORY OF SELF-CONTAINMENT

Most theories of organization discuss how work is divided among units and subunits of bureaucratic structures; several attempt to prescribe one best way of arranging activities; but few anticipate the possible consequences of restructuring or reorganizing work patterns. This is ironic, for the predictive theories we do have—those in which environment, technology, and size are the key independent variables[1]— are of little utility to practicing managers. Once an organization is committed to a set of goals and has established, to use Selznick's phrase, a distinctive competence,[2] little freedom remains to manipulate environment, technology, or, at least in the short run, size. The only thing that can be changed is the internal structure of an organization. Levels of supervision can be added or eliminated; new subunits can be created; and old ones can be absorbed into others. Some consequences of these kinds of structural changes were observed in Chapter 3.

Just as formal positions and lines of authority are variable, so is the degree of interdependence among units in an organization. The effects

[1]See, for example, Paul R. Lawrence and Jay W. Lorsch, *Organization and Environment* (Boston: Harvard Business School, Division of Research, 1967); Joan Woodward, *Industrial Organization: Theory and Practice* (London: Oxford University Press, 1965); William H. Starbuck, "Organizational Growth and Development," in *Handbook of Organizations,* ed. James G. March (Chicago: Rand McNally, 1965), pp. 451-533.
[2]Philip Selznick, *Leadership in Administration* (New York: Harper & Row, 1967), p. 42.

of interdependence are not at all clear, however. In the last chapter it was observed that in the special case of automation, creation of a data-processing staff stimulates establishment of the consultant's or coordinator's role. The coordinator holds a supervisory position, but his real job, it was surmised, is to manage relationships with line managers whose knowledge of the computer is slight. This innovation prevents conflicts between nonexpert managers and expert data-processing specialists of low rank.

In this chapter we shall consider the more general case of interdependence. Interdependence occurs whenever the activities of any unit in an organization are affected by the activities of other units. Interdependence thus gives rise to the need for coordination of activities, whereas the work of independent units does not require coordination. If, for example, a firm were organized into purchasing, manufacturing, and sales divisions, the amount of interdependence among these divisions is considerable. Sales can only sell what manufacturing can produce, and goods can be manufactured only so long as purchasing supplies the needed raw materials. If the major divisions are light bulbs, steam turbines, and submarines, with the purchasing, manufacturing, and sales activities carried out within these units, then interdependence between divisions is minimized. Their activities do not require coordination.

We start from two assumptions about interdependence in organizations. The first is that meaningful differences in the degree of interdependence exist among organizations generally and finance departments in particular. In some departments the flow of work is designed so that units are relatively autonomous, although in others units are required to cooperate with one another. The second assumption is that interdependence is *allocated* in organizations. Put another way, interdependence between units is diminished only at the cost of increasing it within them. The converse also holds. By increasing the extent to which members of a unit must coordinate their activities, interdependence between units is diminished. The assumption that interdependence can be allocated either between or within units holds only so long as an organization's technology does not change fundamentally. Conversion from unit to assembly-line production in a factory, for example, increases interdependence among workmen, as does the introduction of a data-processing section into a formally nonautomated bureaucracy. It should be noted that aside from the impact of automation, the technologies used in finance departments are remarkably similar, as they are simple. The central activities, accounting, collection of funds, approval of disbursements, and postauditing of accounts, are done little differently than they were ten or twenty years ago, and there is little likelihood of major technological breakthroughs.

The theories which discuss interdependence are diverse and sometimes do not speak to one another. Gulick and Urwick have distinguished *purpose* from *process* specialization, pointing out the relative advantages and disadvantages of each. Organization by purpose brings together in one unit all those people who are pursuing a particular goal or providing a service. In finance departments purpose specialization would yield a type of organization not much different from the one reproduced in Figure 1 (in Chapter 1) where the objectives of major subunits are precisely those of the larger organization. Specialization by process would result in a very different formal structure. One division might have charge of maintaining all records, another might be a typing pool, and a machine-accounting or data-processing unit might be present alongside divisions such as accounting and auditing. The benefits of the specialization by purpose, according to Gulick and Urwick, are that it brings together all people needed to accomplish a given task and focuses their activities. A difficulty with this arrangement is that economies of scale may not be realized, and there may not be enough people in each unit to optimize the division of labor or take advantage of the most advanced technologies. However, process specialization also has costs. In particular because it introduces interdependence into organizations the activities of any one unit are affected by the work of others. As Gulick notes, "The necessity of effective coordination is greatly increased . . . a failure in one process affects the whole enterprise and the failure to coordinate one process division may destroy the effectiveness of all the work that is being done."[3]

Simon, Smithburg, and Thompson, while using different language than Gulick and Urwick, draw a similar distinction between organizations where interdependence is present and those where it is minimized or absent. The term *self-contained* is used to describe an organization or

[3]Luther Gulick, "Notes on the Theory of Organization," in *Papers on the Science of Administration,* eds. Luther Gulick and L. Urwick (New York: Institute of Public Administration, 1937), pp. 24-25.

unit of an organization that "depended on no other organization for aid of any kind."[4] Simon *et al.* note that no fully autonomous organizations exist in reality. The difference between self-contained groups and others is therefore relative. In addition, self-contained organizations are usually unitary: They have socially meaningful goals which are thought of as legitimate ends in their own right.[5] The notion of self-containment of organizational units and Gulick and Urwick's concept of specialization of units by purpose are remarkably similar. Process specialization, the obverse of specialization by purpose, thus diminishes self-containment of units because it requires coordination among them.

Like Gulick and Urwick, Simon, Smithburg, and Thompson discuss neither the causes nor consequences of interdependence, but they do indicate a process through which the transition from interdependent to self-contained structures occurs, and also the reverse. Let us consider, to use the language of Simon *et al.*, an organization in which both "line" and "overhead" units are present. This organization is by definition interdependent since the overhead units have no meaningful goals other than aiding the activities of the line departments. (Such an organization is illustrated in Figure 5.) Let us further imagine that a decision is made to reorganize the overhead units so that their activities are carried out within line divisions, rather than separately from them. We can then say that the overhead units have been replaced by auxiliary units within divisions. (Figure 5 also illustrates the new organizational structure.) At the same time this realignment eliminates interdependence between line units since the activities of the former overhead units now take place *within* divisions. In effect, the structure of each line unit comes to resemble closely what the larger organization looked like before the changes occurred. A single unitary organization is replaced by several which report to a common superior. The number of people reporting to the head of the organization is reduced, and spans of control at lower levels are somewhat increased.

Simon, Smithburg, and Thompson's model is based on the experience of public agencies, but a similar process has been noted in business organizations. There are many accounts of the transformation from

[4]Herbert A. Simon, Donald W. Smithburg, and Victor A. Thompson, *Public Administration* (New York: Knopf, 1950), p. 266.
[5]*Ibid.*, p. 268.

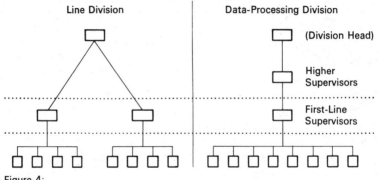

Figure 4:
Two Models of Divisions

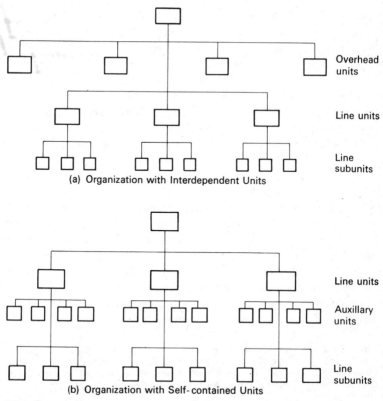

Figure 5:
Interdependent and Self-contained Organizations

"vertical" to "flat" hierarchies which accompanies reorganization from interdependent into largely self-contained units. Typically a firm which is organized into functional units, for instance, purchasing, manufacturing, sales, and so forth, is rearranged so that the major divisions correspond to products or services. Within each of these divisions the pattern of functional organization which characterized the older structure is reproduced, only at a much lower level of hierarchy. Interdependence between divisions decreases substantially as they cease providing services for one another, and separate profit-and-loss figures are computed for each.[6]

A theory of self-containment, or better, an assertion about self-containment is implicit in the works of Gulick and Urwick, Simon et al., and observers of large business enterprises. The assertion is roughly this: Self-containment of organizational units, where desirable, is accomplished through division of one organization into several sub organizations or units which have similar formal structures and which are held together by a common "roof" organization or headquarters office. It is, in short, a theory of organizational mitosis which posits continual division of organizational units into smaller units which come quickly to resemble, in form if not in size, the original one. This theory or assertion appears to be quite plausible, but it raises the question of how organizations maintain their unity. With increasing self-containment, units of organizations become potentially autonomous of one another and of superordinate units. To the extent that organizational units are truly autonomous, a headquarters office, or common superior, to whom they report becomes unnecessary overhead. Very few organizations, however, have rearranged themselves into self-contained units and then dispensed with their higher levels of administration. Indeed, if anything, the opposite tends to have been the case. In business and industrial settings the transformation from functional structures to organizations based on products or profit centers has been accompanied by proliferation of executive offices. The contradiction implicit in the assertion of self-containment—that organizations with fully self-con-

---

[6]See Alfred Chandler, *Strategy and Structure* (Cambridge, Mass.: MIT Press, 1962), and W. Lloyd Warner et al., "The Changing Structure of a Great Corporation," chap. 6 in *The Emergent American Society*, vol. 1, *Large-Scale Organizations* (New Haven, Conn.: Yale University Press, 1967).

tained units cease operating as single organizations—is rarely evidenced in practice.[7]

An entirely different approach to the problem of interdependence among organizational units has been proposed by James D. Thompson. Thompson discusses three types of interdependence: pooled, sequential, and reciprocal. Pooled interdependence is described as a condition where units are autonomous save for the fact that "each part renders a discrete contribution to the whole [organization] and each is supported by the whole."[8] Thompson also speaks of sequential interdependence where the work of one unit of an organization depends on another's activities and, in addition, there is a sequence or time order to activities. To illustrate, the final assembly plant of an automobile manufacturer cannot operate unless engines, drive trains, and other components have been previously built. A third form of interdependence Thompson calls reciprocal; it occurs when "the outputs of each [unit] become inputs for others."[9] Reciprocal interdependence involves two-way interaction between units, whereas the flow of messages is in only one direction where sequential interdependence exists. Thompson notes that the costs of coordination increase as one moves from pooled to sequential to reciprocal interdependence. He posits that under norms of rationality, organizations seek to minimize coordination costs and thus the amount of reciprocal interdependence. One way of doing this is to confine reciprocal interdependence to very small groups, to link these groups together into sequential interdependence, and finally to tie large groups together only in pooled interdependence. Thompson in effect advocates minimization of interdependence and confinement of it within organizational units. Rationality is therefore identified with self-containment. These notions become troublesome because they attribute irrationality to organizations which do not limit reciprocal interdependence to small units and allow only pooled interdependence between large ones. And, in fact, many organizations do not fit Thompson's model. The choice between interdependent and self-

[7]E. Michael Bannister argues that, if anything, self-contained units in business rarely have enough autonomy. See "Multiorganization: Towards a Denouement of The CentDecentRecentralization Imbroglio," *Human Relations*, 23, 1970, 405-429.

[8]James P. Thompson, *Organizations in Action* (New York: McGraw-Hill, 1967), p. 54.

[9]*Ibid.*, p. 55.

contained units is not usually one between irrationality and rationality; surely everyone would opt for that which is rational. Rather, the choice depends on other factors, some of which we will examine in this chapter.

How are these apparently discrepant theories of interdependence in organizations to be reconciled? The classical theorists, Gulick and Urwick and Simon, Smithburg, and Thompson, suggest strongly that self-containment creates powerful centrifugal forces in organizations, whereas James D. Thompson's account leads one to conclude that it is irrational for organizations to discourage self-containment. Let me suggest that the classical theorists, Gulick and Urwick and Simon *et al.*, had a very different conception of organizations than Thompson. The classical theorists were concerned with administration, particularly the broad question of how organizations with vague but complex objectives, such as public bureaucracies, should assign tasks and responsibilities, and make decisions. Absolute rationality does not exist for such organizations; rationality is bounded by the absence of optimal solutions to problems. One must settle for satisfactory accomplishment of ill-defined and sometimes contradictory goals. To be sure, a modicum of efficiency is required, but the survival of administrative structures depends much more on political considerations than on their ability to minimize costs. Thompson, by contrast, draws heavily on the experience of business in formulating his theory. Organizations are expected to be rational and thus strive to develop valid measures of efficiency. Moreover, survival is problematic: "Organizations do some of the basic things they do because they must—or else!"[10] "Or else" reflects the overriding concern for profit in business firms regardless of what they produce or sell. Self-containment of units has a double advantage when units doing different things have the identical objective of profit. Not only are costs of coordination reduced, but the performance of units can be compared because they make independent contributions to profitability, contributions which are "pooled" (to use Thompson's language) to determine the performance of the whole organization.

Self-containment in business organizations leads to greater managerial accountability for the performance of units according to most

[10]*Ibid.*, p. 1.

descriptions. Decentralized control accompanies reorganization into semiautonomous product divisions or profit centers because individual managers can be held responsible for contributing to profitability. Little direct supervision is thus necessary. The expectation that their operations will be profitable, together with the existence of accounting systems which accurately measure each unit's earnings or losses, are assumed to compel behavior consistent with the overall objective of profit.[11] Whether this model of decentralization can be applied to public bureaucracies is a moot question because profitability is rarely a consideration for them. Measures of effectiveness, while important, are elusive when organizational purposes are not easily quantified. Performance or program budgeting which seeks to minimize the cost of providing acceptable levels of service is a partial solution to the problem of devising accounting systems for not-for-profit organizations, but some of the failures of program budgeting have been more conspicuous than the successes.[12] Self-containment of units in bureaucracies, then, does not automatically generate feedback which is useful to top executives as it does in business organizations. This, in turn, suggests that the consequences of self-containment in bureaucracies may be somewhat different than in business settings. Rather than merely resembling the larger structures from which they were formed, self-contained units of bureaucracies may require special mechanisms designed to promote feedback from bottom to top levels, for the absence of these mechanisms may create potential disorganization and endanger organizational coherence.

SELF-CONTAINMENT AND BUREAUCRATIC STRUCTURE

The table of organization of a finance department does not alone reflect the extent to which units are self-contained. Two departments with similar structures may assign responsibilities to units and subunits differently such that one has self-contained units while the other remains interdependent. One must examine what units are doing as well as how they are arranged to estimate the extent of self-containment.

[11]See A. Brown, *Centralized Control with Decentralized Responsibility* (New York: American Management Association, 1927).
[12]See, for example, Robert J. Art, *The TFX Decision* (Boston: Little, Brown, 1968).

Rather than attempting to estimate the degree of self-containment in finance departments, we only separated departments whose units are altogether self-contained from others. Not unexpectedly, a substantial majority of departments fell into the latter group. The procedure used to identify self-contained organizations was simple, if arbitrary. Departments all of whose divisions had financial functions as their primary responsibilities were classified as self-contained. Where one or more divisions were primarily concerned with nonfinancial matters (for example, secretarial, key punching, supplies, duplicating), interdependence was assumed to be present. This classification of department assumes that where goals of all units are organizational goals, interdependence between units is minimized because they need not rely on one another's services. Where, by contrast, the goal of any one unit is not an organizational objective, the unit is assumed to be serving others, and thus interdependent with them. Fifty-two departments were identified as self-contained, leaving 202 with interdependent units.

Identifying the presence or absence of feedback from finance departments was even more difficult than measuring interdependence in them. Feedback is defined as upward communication from the bottom to top levels of hierarchy; it may consist of information about the internal state of an organization or about its environment. Several conditions conducive to upward communication can be identified, but they by no means prove that feedback or upward communication is actually taking place. One is a relatively large proportion of employees whose qualifications are nearly equal to those of managers. If employees at the operating level are to communicate effectively with superiors, their technical knowledge and verbal skills ought to be somewhat greater than employees who are only expected to receive messages and follow instructions. The second condition is open channels of communication. Wide spans of control limit workers' access to supervisors and vice versa, whereas relatively low ratios of subordinates to supervisors promote close contacts. Narrow spans of control would thus contribute to the likelihood of an upward flow of information, though bossism and overbearing supervision are also possible when each supervisor has relatively few subordinates. To summarize, then, feedback is possible, but not demonstrated conclusively, when an organization has many qualified employees and relatively narrow spans of control at lower levels.

Our hypotheses, then, are as follows:

1. Self-containment of units diminishes coordination costs but increases the possibility for disorganization or loss of organizational coherence.

2. In business organizations self-containment allows calculation of the profit (or loss) of each unit, which in turn permits accurate appraisal and comparisons of performance, but similar measures of performance do not exist for bureaucracies because of their multiple and ill-defined objectives.

3. Special feedback mechanisms must therefore be devised in self-contained bureaucracies if disorganization or loss of coherence are to be averted; these mechanisms include communication patterns which allow an upward flow of messages and large numbers of expert employees.

4. Self-containment in bureaucracies is thus associated with mechanisms promoting feedback, in particular low spans of control within divisions of departments, and high educational qualifications among employees.

The data on finance departments, it turns out, do not entirely confirm these hypotheses. They suggest rather that self-containment triggers a complex, and perhaps contradictory, set of changes in organizations. Mechanisms promoting feedback apparently emerge with self-containment, but other structural changes occur which nearly obscure these effects.

The formal structure of finance departments with entirely self-contained units is very different from the interdependent departments. Table 8 presents data for whole departments; divisions are described in Table 9. It should first be noted that no relationship appears between organizational size and self-containment. Fourteen of the sixty-four smallest departments, eleven of those with thirty-five to fifty-nine employees, twenty-one with sixty to one hundred members, and only six of sixty-two with one hundred or more employees are classified as self-contained. The absence of a linear association between size and self-containment raises some questions about classical theories such as Gulick and Urwick's. The major disadvantage of self-containment, they claim, is that economies of scale may not be realized. Large organizations presumably realize economies of scale more easily than small

Table 8

Structural Differentiation by Self-Containment, Controlling for Size
(Means and Standard Errors)

	Number of Employees			
	20-34	35-59	60-99	100+
Levels of Hierarchy				
In interdependent departments	3.36	3.57	3.95	4.64
Error	0.08	0.07	0.11	0.14
N	(50)	(53)	(43)	(56)
In self-contained departments	4.01	3.96	3.99	5.00
Error	0.22	0.25	0.16	0.45
N	(14)	(11)	(21)	(6)
Operating Divisions				
In interdependent departments	4.88	5.59	6.09	8.04
Error	0.23	0.20	0.34	0.52
N	(50)	(53)	(43)	(56)
In self-contained departments	2.71	3.82	4.81	6.67
Error	0.30	0.40	0.38	0.56
N	(14)	(11)	(21)	(6)
Span of Control of First-Line Supervisors				
In interdependent departments	4.15	5.46	6.69	11.71
Error	0.26	0.39	0.36	1.00
N	(50)	(53)	(43)	(55)
In self-contained departments	5.54	5.62	8.05	10.00
Error	0.89	0.95	0.83	2.36
N	(14)	(11)	(21)	(6)
Span of Control of Intermediate Supervisors				
In interdependent departments	1.24	1.58	1.72	2.08
Error	0.08	0.12	0.15	0.10
N	(43)	(46)	(40)	(55)
In self-contained departments	1.73	1.70	1.99	2.10
Error	0.37	0.20	0.25	0.20
N	(13)	(11)	(21)	(6)
Proportion of Employees Expected to Have A.B. Degree				
In interdependent departments	0.248	0.232	0.237	0.297
Error	0.021	0.023	0.018	0.018
N	(50)	(53)	(43)	(56)
In self-contained departments	0.287	0.389	0.310	0.542
Error	0.051	0.039	0.048	0.068
N	(14)	(11)	(21)	(6)

ones. One would therefore expect self-containment to appear most often in large organizations, but the data on finance departments suggest that this is not the case.

Self-containment, however, is significantly associated with variations in the formal structure of finance departments. A decreasing number of units reporting to the head of the organization is anticipated by traditional notions about self-containment, but the proliferation of levels is not. Of departments with fewer than thirty-five members, those with interdependent units have a mean of 4.88 divisions, while the mean number of divisions is only 2.71 where units are entirely self-contained. Differences of this magnitude hold regardless of departmental size: 5.59 compared with 3.82 in departments with thirty-five to fifty-nine members, 6.09 versus 4.81 in departments with sixty to one hundred members, and 8.04 compared with 6.67 in the largest finance agencies with more than one hundred members. At the same time, the number of hierarchical levels generally increases with self-containment, from 3.36 to 4.01 where there are fewer than thirty-five employees, from 3.57 to 3.96 in the next largest group of departments, and from 4.64 to 5.00 in the larger departments. (Among agencies with sixty to ninety-nine members, self-containment makes no significant difference in the number of hierarchical levels.) Self-containment, then, is associated with tall structures which are compressed at the top, whereas interdependent departments tend to be short and somewhat wide at the top levels.

The third and fourth panels of Table 8 show the effects of self-containment on spans of control when size is controlled. Self-containment increases ratios of subordinates to supervisors at the lowest and intermediate levels, but the differences are small and statistically significant for only three of eight possible comparisons. For example, in the smallest departments, spans of control average 4.15 at the lowest level and 1.24 at intermediate levels when divisions are interdependent. With self-containment, however, spans of control rise to 5.54 and 1.73, respectively. The only other significant difference occurs among departments with sixty to ninety-nine employees; the span of control of first-line supervisors increases from 6.69 to 8.05 with self-containment. These data when considered together with data on the number of division heads reporting to the head of the department reveal an intriguing pattern, however. Among the smallest departments, those with interdependent units have a mean of 4.88 divisions and spans of control of 4.15 at the bottom, roughly equal ratios of subordinates to supervisors at the highest and lowest levels. With self-containment, the department heads' span of control drops to 2.71 while the first-line span of control increases to 5.54. A similar pattern occurs among agencies with sixty to ninety-nine members. With interdependence the spans of control are 6.09 at the highest level and 6.69 at the lowest level, but when units are self-contained these figures change to 4.81 and 8.05, respectively. Self-containment, then, leads organizations to contact at top levels but bulge at the bottom. This runs contrary to our earlier prediction that spans of control would decrease with self-containment, and it would seem to confirm the model of self-containment implicit in classical theories of administrative behavior. Indeed, the main effect of self-containment seems to be to transfer some positions, presumably those occupied by clerical and support personnel, from high to low levels. This is not inconsistent with Thompson's theory; the proliferation of lower-level positions associated with self-containment suggests that interdependence is being confined within units rather than taking place between them. But whether this decreases costs of communication and coordination and leads to decentralization in bureaucracies is another matter.

Self-containment and Centralization

In a sentence, these data provide no evidence whatsoever that self-containment is conducive to decentralized decision making or rules and regulations which remove authority from the managerial hierarchy among the 254 departments of finance. The self-contained finance agencies are no more, and no less, likely to delegate decision-making authority or to rely on impersonal means of evaluation than interdependent departments. This holds whether or not size and other variables are controlled.[13] Self-containment and confinement of interdependence to small units do not lead to decentralization in bureaucracies, we would argue, because the contradiction in the classical theories mentioned earlier—organizations with self-contained units cease to be single organizations—reflects an administrative reality in bureaucratic structures. If an interdependent bureaucracy is divided into several

---

[13]There is in fact a slight but nonsignificant tendency for self-contained departments to be *more* centralized than interdependent ones, when other variables are controlled.

unitary, self-contained units and decision-making authority altogether decentralized, nothing remains for the larger organization to do. Its units are pursuing disparate goals, not a common objective which would allow the "pooling" of accomplishments; no justification for maintaining the larger organization remains. What is rational for business firms pursuing profit, above all, reorganization into self-contained units, may be something less than rational for organizations involved mainly in administrative activities. But there is yet another paradox to be explored.

A PARADOX: SELF-CONTAINMENT, EXPERTNESS, AND THE SPAN OF CONTROL

The bottom panel of Table 8 shows proportions of employees of finance departments who are expected to have college degrees or equivalent work experience. Such employees we will call "experts" even though their formal qualifications may have little to do with the work in which they are engaged. Save for the largest departments, agencies with interdependent structures expect college degrees of about a quarter of their members, but this proportion ranges from 29 to 39 percent where units are self-contained. And among the largest finance offices, about 30 percent of employees in interdependent departments are expected to have a degree, but this increases to 54 percent in departments where units are self-contained. A modest association between self-containment and the qualifications expected of employees is indicated. But even more interesting is the impact of employees' qualifications on the formal structure of finance departments.

If one assumes that one function of expert employees is to provide feedback for managers, it follows that experts will need open channels of communication, hence relatively many supervisors. To test this notion requires data on divisions, not whole departments, for communication would be most intense in parts of organizations where the most experts work. For each finance department two sets of data describing its divisions were computed. One set includes divisions in which more than one-quarter of the employees hold positions for which a college degree is expected; these divisions have high proportions of experts. Other divisions in which one-quarter or fewer of employees have jobs for which a degree is expected are considered to have low proportions of experts. In 37 of the 254 agencies, no divisions expected college training of more than a quarter of their members, and in six departments *all* divisions expect such high qualifications.

Table 9 makes it clear that when one compares units within departments, those with high proportions of expert employees have much narrower spans of control for first-line supervisors than where few experts are present, 8.37 compared with 4.86. Furthermore, as the second panel of the table shows, the difference between expert and nonexpert divisions holds when departmental size is controlled. In the smaller departments, those with fewer than 60 employees, spans of control drop from 5.56 to 3.34 as expertness increases, and the drop is from 11.27 to 6.25 in the larger departments. There is also some evidence that spans of control at intermediate levels drop, from 1.60 to 1.28, as employees' qualifications increase, but this difference all but

Table 9
Spans of Control of First-Line Supervisors by Expertness and Self-containment (Means and Standard Errors)

	In Divisions with Few Experts	In Divisions with Many Experts
In all departments	8.37	4.86
Error	0.40	0.34
N	(248)	(217)
In departments with 20-59 employees	5.56	3.34
Error	0.32	0.31
N	(126)	(104)
In departments with 60+ employees	11.27	6.25
Error	0.67	0.56
N	(122)	(113)
In departments with inter-dependent units	8.41	4.57
Error	0.47	0.35
N	(200)	(175)
In departments with self-contained units	8.18	6.06
Error	0.69	1.03
N	(48)	(42)

disappears when size is controlled. Three variables, self-containment, expertness, and spans of control, are thus associated in a puzzling fashion. We had hypothesized that self-containment in bureaucracies gives rise to mechanisms which promote feedback: expert employees and narrow spans of control. Indeed, the data show that finance agencies with self-contained units have more qualified personnel than others. Expertness decreases spans of control also as expected, but despite this, self-containment *increases* somewhat the number of subordinates per supervisor. In the third panel of Table 9 spans of control at the lowest level of bureaucracies are related to both expertness and self-containment. Expertness decreases spans of control here as before but the effect is much smaller, from 8.18 to 6.06, in self-contained agencies than in interdependent ones, where the decrease is from 8.41 to 4.57. At the same time, self-containment increases spans of control, but only in units that have many experts. Self-containment, then, promotes the use of expert employees which in turn diminishes spans of control at the lowest level. The direct effect of self-containment, however, is to increase spans of control. Both the classical theory of self-containment, which anticipates the increasing spans of control at the lower levels of an organization, and our prediction of a narrowing hierarchy seem partly correct, but for different reasons. Self-containment contracts organizations at top levels but expands them at the bottom simply because some offices are moved from higher to lower levels. At the same time, the need for feedback from self-contained units of bureaucracies brings in more expert employees and narrows spans of control; this all but masks the increased number of lower-level employees caused by self-containment itself.

BUREAUCRATIC VERSUS ECONOMIC MODELS OF RATIONALITY

The findings reviewed in this chapter and the previous one indicate that interdependence and self-containment have quite different effects on the structure of bureaucratic organizations. At least in the case of automation, interdependence gives rise to coordination of activities of organizational units. Self-containment, by contrast, is accompanied by mechanisms which promote feedback. These structural innovations are quite different—one stimulates horizontal communication, the other vertical communication—but both are in response to an organizational imperative which, it may be surmised, holds for all bureaucratic systems. This imperative is the need to avoid conflict or disorganization or to maintain what I call *organizational coherence*: the sense that the dispersed parts of an organization are pursuing common rather than disparate ends and that they are doing so cooperatively rather than antagonistically. Interdependence is a potential threat to coherence because it introduces nonhierarchical relationships between high-status nonexperts and low-status experts into organizations. The coordinator's role emerges in response to this problem. Self-containment potentially damages coherence because it allows units of an organization extreme autonomy in the absence of common objectives or criteria by which the performance of units can be compared. Efforts are therefore made to stimulate feedback from bottom to top levels. Organizational coherence is not to be equated with economic rationality, narrowly conceived. Economic rationality, the logic of efficiency, demands that coordination costs be minimized. The coordinator's role, if anything, increases costs. Economic rationality demands that vertical communication and the ratio of supervisors to subordinates be minimized, but feedback mechanisms which accompany self-containment tend to do just the opposite. The logic of efficiency, thus, is a poor guide to the behavior of bureaucratic organizations. The imperative of coordination, the need to maintain organizations *as such*, must be satisfied too.

An emphasis on economic rationality has pervaded the literature on organizations, almost to the exclusion of fundamental sociological considerations. It has given rise to two popular misconceptions. One is that rationality in the design of organizations requires consideration of only technological and environmental demands. Self-maintenance needs of organizations are considered relatively unimportant. The second is that rationality in bureaucratic systems gives rise to patterns of authority characterized by domination and subordination, whereas this is not the case where the profit motive prevails. These views have very different origins: The first is a product of an approach to organizations which emphasizes decision making and reconciliation of "closed-system" and "open-system" models, while the second derives from a body of conservative political doctrine which stresses the primacy of economic values in human behavior. But they hold in common the notion that a utilitarian calculus ultimately governs organizations whether this is in terms of minimizing costs or maximizing profits.

Let us first consider the notion that technology and environment alone determine the structure of organizations. James D. Thompson writes:

> . . . organizational rationality involves three major component activities: (1) input activities, (2) technological activities, and (3) output activities. Since these are interdependent, organizational rationality requires that they be appropriately geared to one another. The inputs acquired must be within the scope of the technology, and it must be within the capacity of the organization to dispose of the technological production.[14]

This view of rationality approaches tautology, of course. To say that inputs, technology, and outputs must be "geared" to one another admits to many meanings. More important, however, is that the problem of disorganization or of organizational coherence is never mentioned in connection with rationality. As a result some propositions are developed which do not altogether fit our findings. One of Thompson's propositions which we have already noted states that "under norms of rationality, organizations group positions to minimize coordination costs."[15] Were this true we would find minimal interdependence between organizational units, but in fact this is not the case. Our findings suggest that coordination costs can be diminished in bureaucracies, but this economy is at least partly offset by the effort required to secure more intense feedback which is needed to preserve coherence once units become self-contained. Similarly, Thompson posits that "under norms of rationality, organizations facing heterogeneous task environments seek to identify homogenous segments and establish structural units to deal with each."[16] To establish a separate structural unit for each element in the environment may make sense in the short run, but the long-run risk of having these units coopted by clients or suppliers is great.[17] If the present analysis is correct, communications between these units and top managers must be intense to preserve their identification with the larger organization. This, of course, has economic costs which may possibly exceed the benefits of establishing the separate units in the first place. In general, administrative rationality in Thompson's model is identified with cutting costs of communication

---

[14]Thompson, *Organizations in Action*, p. 19.
[15]*Ibid.*, p. 57.
[16]*Ibid.*, p. 70.
[17]Cooptation is discussed in Philip Selznick, *TVA and the Grass Roots* (Berkeley: University of California Press, 1949), expecially pp. 259-261.

both within an organization and between an organization and its environment, thus diminishing communication itself. This, in turn, limits an organization's ability to elicit cooperation and behavior consistent with objectives from its members. The effects of this on organizational coherence are fairly obvious.

The notion that bureaucracy entails domination and subordination is an old one; it is part of the verbal ordinance used by conservative critics of "big government" and of socialism in particular. Nonetheless, it has elements of the theory of organization which ought to be examined here. One of the most outspoken of the neoclassical economists, von Mises, describes bureaucratic management as:

> ... management bound to comply with detailed rules and regulations fixed by the authority of a superior body. The task of the bureaucrat is to perform what these rules and regulations order him to do. His discretion to act according to his own best conviction is seriously restricted by them.
>
> Business management or profit management is management directed by the profit motive. The objective of business management is to make a profit. As success or failure to attain this end can be ascertained by accounting not only for the whole business concern but also for any of its parts, it is feasible to decentralize both management and accountability without jeopardizing the unity of operations and the attainment of their goal. Responsibility can be divided. There is no need to limit the discretion of subordinates by any rules or regulations other than that underlying all business activities, namely, to render their operations profitable.
>
> The objectives of public administration cannot be measured in money terms and cannot be checked by accountancy methods.[18]

This criticism of bureaucracy, then, posits close supervision and detailed rules and codes which all but eliminate discretion as the only alternative to a utilitarian calculus in organizations. The former are identified with bureaucratic management, and the latter with profit management, of course. The question raised here is whether another form of administration is possible, one which relies on intensive communication between managers and groups of expert subordinates working in self-contained units which have socially meaningful goals. In place of domination and subordination, detailed information about objectives and decision premises are transmitted to lower levels, and

[18]Ludwig von Mises, *Bureaucracy* (New Haven, Conn.: Yale University Press, 1944), pp. 45-46.

feedback about performance is funneled upward. The logic of this pattern is precisely the logic of the decentralized business enterprise, only the objectives and decision premises involved are much more complex. Bureaucratic organization, so managed, is not a cheap form of administration. Indeed, the use of arbitrary rules and domination is probably the least expensive way to administer organizations whose goals are complex and not readily understood by employees. Nonetheless, the model we have proposed is an alternative to old-fashioned bureaucracy envisioned by von Mises, and it is a model toward which profit-oriented organizations may have to move as noneconomic considerations are forced upon them.

There has been much advocacy of self-containment of units in business organizations. Phrases such as "management by objectives" are used to describe behavior patterns that supposedly develop once a table of organization is rearranged so that the objectives of all units are identical with organizational goals themselves. Once made aware of objectives, it is argued, people more or less automatically behave in a rational, goal-directed manner that allows reduction of costs of supervision and of coordination. This may be the case in business settings (we have no evidence to suggest otherwise), but if it is true, it is because business must first show a satisfactory return on investment before satisfying other considerations. It is not the absence of the profit motive of bureaucracies, but rather the complexity (and occasional uncertainty) of objectives that precludes any simple nostrums for inefficiency, real or imagined. Self-containment of units in bureaucracies as elsewhere reduces interdependence between units and probably has the advantage of focusing people's attention on objectives rather than processes. But it has other consequences, the most important being the need for increased feedback which entails hiring expert employees and increasing the relative number of supervisory positions somewhat. Self-containment may be associated with higher *quality* administration, but we have no way of knowing this for sure. The present analysis shows only that self-containment has multiple consequences for organizational structure, some anticipated by traditional theories, some not.

6
Toward a Sociological Theory of Organizations

This last chapter will raise two questions that should be asked of all social science research. One is the matter of reasonableness: Do the data and interpretations of them make sense? To be sure, we cannot disregard rigorous methodologies, but findings from exploratory research based on small, nonrandom samples are necessarily suspect if they lack face validity. A second question concerns meaning or relevance. The line separating trivia from insights fraught with meaning is again a subjective one. The sociologist's art consists of finding meaning, of connecting bits of data to some of the larger issues that have occupied scholars and social critics over the years.

Let me indicate how the questions of reasonableness and relevance will be handled. To establish reasonableness, I will first list the empirical findings reported in this book and alongside them inferences drawn from the findings. The inferences are more important than the findings themselves, so the test of face validity should be applied to them. I will then turn to an informal study of business firms I did in 1968 as a further test of these inferences. The interviews suggest more similarities between corporate giants and small bureaucracies than are usually imagined. The question of relevance or of meaning very much concerns me, but I am also concerned that "relevance" has become a fad and a cover used to avoid some very difficult questions facing social science. The most consistent impression one gains from this research is that social systems tend to change only in complex and incremental ways, or not at all. This is nothing new, but it acquires importance when applied to organizations which are supposedly rational in their pursuit of concrete ends. And it is doubly important when we realize that such inertia, at least among public bureaucracies, is a function of structural exigencies, not individual motives. Identifying and quantifying these exigencies should be the first task of social science. This study may also be judged relevant if it helps crystallize some ideas about the possibility for individual autonomy in organizational settings. The last section consists of some informed speculations about this, which, I believe, would have no credibility but for the empirical research that preceded it.

SUMMARY OF FINDINGS

The findings from this study are diverse, and no attempt will be made to subsume them under one or two broad theoretical generalizations. A theoretical *perspective* will be emphasized here, but that is very different from a set of propositions which logically follow from one another. The findings can be grouped under two headings, effects of organizational size and shape of the hierarchy, and effects of interdependence or its obverse, self-containment.

Size is of fundamental importance in organizations. Values of many variables describing organizational attributes (for example, number of levels, number of subunits, number of sections, ratio of subordinates to supervisors) increase with size, but whether this reflects causal connections or sheer tautology is not known. Only careful longitudinal studies will reveal what, if any, causal pattern can be imputed to these associations, and there has been almost no research of this sort.[1] Given the high likelihood of tautology, significance was attached only to findings that were patently nontautological. One datum worthy of attention was the extremely narrow spans of control at intermediate levels of finance departments. The data also revealed that very large departments have about three times as many intermediate levels with narrow spans of control than the smallest departments. Furthermore, supervisors at these levels spend more of their time supervising, broadly defined, than their counterparts at the operating level. It was surmised

[1]Longitudinal analysis of the data collected in 1966 and further data collected in 1971 suggests that size is indeed the causal variable. See Marshall W. Meyer, "Size and the Structure of Organizations: A Causal Analysis," *American Sociological Review*, 37, 1972.

that planning and evaluation of others' work rather than direct supervision occupy much of the time of supervisors at intermediate levels. This, in turn, was taken as evidence of separation of nonoperational from operational goals, which March and Simon assert to be characteristic of all organizations. The data suggest that, by contrast, ends and means are distinguished in large departments but not in small ones. Our inference was that increasing size compels separation of nonoperational from operational goals, if only to avoid rigid centralization, and this in turn has ramifications for authority practices. "Strict super- and subordination" no longer holds where managers have responsibility for transforming abstract goals into operational programs of behavior for subordinates. Increased size, then, appears to be associated with movement away from the idea of an inflexible chain of command, at least for workers at intermediate levels of hierarchy. It is not clear that this pattern extends to the operating level however.

The effects of an organization's shape, whether horizontally or vertically differentiated, on authority practices were also examined. Net of size, the more subunits in an organization, the greater the likelihood of centralized decision making and of rules and regulations that allow discretion to top managers. The more hierarchical levels, net of size, the greater the likelihood of decentralization of decisions and of rules and regulations that constrain decisions in advance, removing authority from the managerial hierarchy. Other research, particularly the work of the Aston group, has suggested similar relationships,[2] and the Carzo and Yanouzas experiment indicated that decision processes vary systematically with group structure in a manner consistent with our data. Several inferences were derived from these findings. One is that centralized control and authoritative regulations are functional alternatives. A second, derived from the first, posits an equilibrium between forces that would centralize and forces that would disperse authority in organizations, and argues that in the absence of such equilibrium, organizational effectiveness may be impaired.

Interdependence and self-containment describe the flow of work in organizations, not formal structure, but they have implications for structure. Interdependence exists when one unit's activities depend on

---

[2]See D. S. Pugh et al., "Dimensions of Organizational Structure," *Administrative Science Quarterly,* 13, 1968, 65-105 and especially table 4, p. 83, which presents correlations among scales measuring organization structure.

another's; self-containment of units renders them autonomous./We/ assumed that the presence of a data-processing unit in an organization stimulates interdependence, bringing high-status nonexperts and low-status data-processing specialists into nonhierarchical relationships and creating potential for conflict. It was further assumed that structural adjustments are made in the face of these difficulties. Data-processing divisions, the analysis indicates, are organized very differently from others. They have more levels of hierarchy, narrower spans of control at intermediate levels, and wider spans of control at the operating level than others. Furthermore, supervisors at intermediate levels spend less time supervising than their counterparts at the operating level, a reversal of the usual pattern. These findings suggest that data-processing units tend to have high-status supervisory positions to which few supervisory duties are attached. The inference is that managers in these positions have responsibility for coordination of nonhierarchical relationships with other units. Interdependence between units thus gives rise to coordination of activities.

Self-containment, by contrast, has very different consequences. Self-containment promotes autonomy of units but does not automatically generate feedback from them in bureaucracies as it does in business. Mechanisms promoting feedback are therefore necessary, among them employees with high qualifications and open channels of communication which presumably exist when spans of control are narrow. The data showed that departments with self-contained units have more qualified employees than interdependent departments. Furthermore, spans of control decrease sharply as employees' qualifications increase. Nonetheless, the simple effect of self-containment is to increase spans of control slightly if not significantly. Self-containment, by moving some units from top to bottom levels of organizations, necessarily increases spans of control at the operating level, but the need for feedback is met by adding expert employees and narrowing spans of control; the two effects nearly cancel one another. The inference here is like one drawn earlier: An equilibrium exists between forces that would disperse and forces that would centralize organizations. Conflicts arising between interdependent units could be left to fester, but the coordinator's role emerges instead. Self-contained units could be allowed autonomy, but feedback from them is encouraged to preserve their ties with the larger organization/What I have called/organizational coherence is maintained; equilibrium rather than instability characterizes bureaucratic structures. The findings and inferences drawn from them are summarized in Table 10.

In addition to suggesting the existence of equilibria, the data also indicate that relationships among variables describing organizations are rarely simple. If there is a general pattern, it is that variations in organizational structure have multiple and inconsistent effects. The direct effect of increased size, we surmised, is to promote economies in supervision, but the indirect effect is to decrease such economies because of added intermediate supervisory levels. Vertical differentiation leads simultaneously to decentralization and rules that largely determine decisions in advance; horizontal differentiation has the opposite effects. Self-containment has the direct effect of increasing spans of control, but because it is accompanied by higher qualifications for employees its indirect effect is to decrease spans of control. To say that organizations or social systems in general are complex is not a theory. Indeed, it may impede theorizing. But it may be an accurate description of how organizations actually function. Ironic as it seems, the only underlying simplicity may be pervasive complexity.

AN EXCURSION INTO INDUSTRY

The 254 departments of finance are a small and unrepresentative sample of the organizations in the United States or elsewhere, yet the arguments made here are stated as if they apply to all organizations. The extent to which the findings can be generalized may never be known, but it is possible to judge whether the results presented here are altogether peculiar to finance departments. One way of doing this is to use what Przeworski and Teune call the "most different systems" method.[3] The technique involves comparisons of social systems at any level of analysis—organizations, communities, or whole societies—which are maximally different with respect to theoretically significant variables. Should similar patterns of *relationships* among variables hold across maximally different systems, it is presumed that these relationships hold for all systems. If, for example, one wants to test the generality of findings from a study of small, not-for-profit organiza-

[3]Adam Przeworski and Henry Teune, *The Logic of Comparative Social Inquiry* (New York: Wiley, 1970), chap. 2.

Table 10
Summary of Findings and Inferences

Findings	Inferences
Chapter	
2. Greater size is accompanied by increased numbers of supervisory levels and wider spans of control at all levels. Spans of control at intermediate levels are much smaller than elsewhere, regardless of size, but intermediate supervisors supervise more than others.	Large organizations separate non-operational from operational goals whereas small organizations tend not to do this. Relationships between workers on different levels are characterized by efforts to translate abstract ends into concrete means in large organizations, whereas the exercise of face-to-face authority and subordination persists in small organizations.
3. Horizontal differentiation is associated with centralization of decisions and rules that centralize discretion in the managerial hierarchy. Vertical differentiation is associated with decentralization of decisions and rules that remove discretion from managers.	Decentralization of authority to make decisions is accompanied by rules and regulations that largely determine decisions in advance. Centralization of authority in the managerial hierarchy and centralization of discretion in authoritative rules are thus functional alternatives.
4. Data-processing divisions have more levels of hierarchy, narrower spans of control at intermediate levels, and wider spans of control at the lowest level than other divisions. In data-processing divisions, first-line supervisors spend more time supervising than in other divisions, but intermediate supervisors spend less time supervising than elsewhere.	The presence of a data-processing staff creates interdependence in organizations, requiring cooperation between managers who know little about automated processes and data-processing experts of low rank. The potential for conflict in such non-hierarchical relationships is high, hence the coordinator's or consultant's role (a supervisory position with few supervisory duties) emerges to manage these relationships.
5. Self-containment of units is associated with high educational qualifications among employees; high educational requirements are in turn associated with narrow spans of control. Holding educational requirements constant, self-containment increases spans of control somewhat.	Unlike in business, self-containment does not automatically generate feedback in bureaucracies, hence mechanisms promoting feedback (highly qualified employees and narrow spans of control) are needed. Such mechanisms appear, but they are masked by increasing of spans of control at the operating level which accompany self-containment because some units are moved from higher to lower levels.

tions, he would test his hypotheses on a set of large, profit-oriented, if not profit-making, firms. This is precisely what I did during the summer of 1968.

The less said about the twelve corporations in this informal study, the better, because much of what was told me was sensitive, if not confidential. The twelve were randomly selected from the top of the *Fortune* "500" list of the largest U.S. industrial firms. Some of the corporations are quite old and have felt little of the impact of automation and other technological advances; others are inextricably tied to the most modern technologies. Interviews were conducted with several executives in each firm (usually a vice president in charge of administration and one or two of his assistants) and covered topics including the administrative structure of the firm, delegation of decision-making authority, evaluation and compensation of executives, and past and anticipated changes in patterns or organization. No fixed questionnaire was used, but the same list of topics was covered in all twelve firms. Each interview consumed the better part of an eight-hour day, including a trip to the executive dining room in several cases. In addition to taking notes, I tape recorded the interviews. Transcriptions of these recordings provided most of the descriptive material that follows.

Not all the hypotheses suggested by the study of finance departments could be tested with the data on corporations, but two of the most interesting ones can be reexamined. One is the relationship between formal structure, decision making, and procedures used in evaluating personnel. Official tables of organization describe the actual lines of authority among executives. In some corporations as few as six persons report directly to the president, while in others the number is as high as twenty-one. Perhaps of more significance is whether the distinction between line and staff units is maintained. In three firms there was no such distinction, more likely than not because only one unit in each (called operations or manufacturing) could conceivably be called line, and even this would be misleading. Tables of organization conventionally place line units directly below the chief executive and staff units to the side. In the three firms which did not divide line from staff, all units fall below the president's office; none serves only in an advisory capacity. The other nine firms do not follow this practice.

The degree of centralization or decentralization is not as explicitly stated by the firms, but the interviews suggest three different patterns. Highly centralized control characterizes three of the corporations, not surprisingly the same three which had no line-staff distinction. Executives in these firms indicated that very little discretion was allowed to department and division chiefs. In one, nonbudgeted expenditures over $5000 required approval of the board of directors. In another, a preference for short lines of communication was voiced. This meant that in practice the president or one of his assistants would intervene, usually by telephone, to resolve relatively minor questions. In the third, the rules governing decisions were unclear, but few deviations from budgets are permitted. A second pattern of decision making I label mixed; it reflects partial, but by no means full, decentralization. There are actually two forms of mixed decision making. In one form, staff units have power of review or concurrence over decisions made at lower levels. The mixed pattern is also judged present when corporate commitments are made centrally but executed on a decentralized basis. The third type of decision making is full decentralization. The four decentralized corporations are split into autonomous self-contained profit centers, from as few as four to as many as seventy of them. Each profit center has responsibility for manufacturing and selling its products and for showing a satisfactory return on the firm's investment. Typically, managers of profit centers are two or three levels removed from the head of the organization and can authorize expenditures of from $50,000 to $100,000 which are not anticipated by budgets. The procedures used in evaluating executives are not classified here, but they are easily summarized as in Table 11.

Table 11 displays characteristics of the formal structure, decision making, and evaluation procedures in the twelve firms. At first glance, the association between the number of units reporting directly to the president and centralization of authority appears degenerate. If one eliminates staff units from consideration, however, the most centralized firms have the greatest number of units at the second level. The relationship between centralization and horizontal differentiation at the second level becomes even sharper when we note that eight of the staff units in corporation D are called "operations staff": They are quasi-line units. Some similarity between huge corporations and departments of finance is thus suggested. And the similarity is further suggested by the correspondence between evaluation procedures and styles of decision

Table 11
Decision-Making, Structure, and Evaluation Procedures in Twelve Corporations

Corporation	Units	Decision-Making	Evaluation
A	13*	Centralized	Qualitative.
B	12*	Centralized	Qualitative — on "overall performance." Informal methods preferred.
C	12*	Centralized	In terms of deviations from standard costs of budget estimates.
D	3 line 14 staff	Mixed	"Brownie point" system, otherwise indescribable. (Had not been implemented at time of interview.)
E	4 line 5 staff	Mixed	In terms of accomplishment of goals. Goals are *not* directly related to revenues and profits, however.
F	3 line 7 staff	Mixed	"Sign-ups" — new business most important. Also in terms of revenues and profits.
G	3 line 3 staff	Mixed	Qualitative; some attempt to assess contribution to profit.
H	4 line 8 staff	Mixed	Sales, profits, and new business acquisitions.
J	7 line 14 staff	Decentralized	Performance of unit; accomplishment.
K	5 line 12 staff	Decentralized	Qualitative and in terms of personal objectives.
L	4 line 5 staff	Decentralized	Performance of divisions and departments.
M	2 line 4 staff	Decentralized	"Accomplishments, performance. We actually get each year a written list of accomplishments of each guy."

*No distinction between line and staff units.

making. Two of the three centralized firms rely on only qualitative indicators of performance, usually a supervisor's judgment, and one of the two does not have written instructions to guide supervisors' evaluations. Three of the four fully decentralized corporations, by contrast, evaluate managers strictly in terms of performance: contributions to sales, profit, and long-term growth of the business. Where the mixed pattern of decision making prevails, a variety of evaluative procedures are used. The "brownie point" system about to be inaugurated in company D defied comprehension; a myriad of data about each executive was to be analyzed to produce an overall ranking. Corporation E had a "goals program," but it was admitted that the goals in terms of which managers were evaluated may have had no relationship, or even an adverse relationship, to profit. And both companies F and H were more concerned with new business than profitability. The partly decentralized firms, in other words, had more or less quantitative indicators of performance, but their connection to the objective of maximizing return on investment was tenuous. Evaluation procedures among corporations as among finance departments vary with formal structure and the degree of centralization of authority. Decentralization is accompanied by impersonal, quantitiative criteria for assessing performance which leave little direction to managers, whereas qualitative judgments are made in the centralized firms.

A second inference, the notion of coherence or equilibrium in organizations, can be partly examined with the data on corporations. In Chapter 3 we spoke of a balance between forces that would centralize and forces that would disperse organizations. And in Chapter 5 it was surmised that, at least among bureaucracies, self-containment creates potential for considerable autonomy for units, so mechanisms promoting feedback develop in the absence of valid measures of performance. Like the finance departments, corporations appear to find self-containment a mixed blessing. The three centralized firms have not changed their structures appreciably in recent years, but the other nine have experimented with varying degrees of self-containment and decentralization. *Of the nine, four now allow units less autonomy than they did ten years ago.* One of these corporations remains fully decentralized, but fewer and larger profit centers than before now exist. The other three have eliminated self-contained units completely. A number of economic factors were cited as causes of recentralization, but beneath them lies another reason. As several informants put it, "We lost control." Excerpts from two interviews demonstrate this point vividly.

> The fundamental, the last major change made in the company or organization goes back to 19__ when the company was first divisionalized. Following that we went through about a three-year period of trying to understand what we decided to do. There was a tremendous amount of sorting out necessary.
>
> (What was the organization of the company like before it was divisionalized?)
>
> It was almost like a current division. It was functionally organized— we had a vice president of manufacturing and he ran manufacturing for the whole company. They had a vice president of engineering and he ran engineering for the whole company. Very analogous to our current divisions. The fundamental reason for divisionalizing at that point was just to be able to cope with the volume of activity that we were driving up on. We couldn't do it in one very large organization. We had to have some project, some program specialization; it was too unwieldy. We went through about a three-year period, as I said, trying to sort out what that meant. During that period I think we suffered the pendulum swinging too far in the direction of decentralization. This word "autonomy" got involved in people's thinking.
>
> (In what way did it hurt the company?)
>
> I think in fact what did hurt the company during that period was a loss of this centralized commitment control. Loss of control over basic business commitments, that is, to the divisions. I don't mean to be critical of divisions, they had justifications for thinking the way they did. They were thinking they were autonomous profit-making centers and that if they chose to invest money in facilities, to invest money in research, or commit to a new product development, that was their perogative as long as they made money, Whether or not we make money is kind of a fifteen-year span on any given program, and their view and their longevity isn't that long. *The corporation lost control* of making those fundamental commitments during that period. . . .
>
> With the geography and everything else at the time, these distribution warehouses—they were called warehouses and they had certain territories—had almost complete autonomy. They bought ___ and they bought ___, and they bought any other things that they thought would go with it in their business. They sold to other people, they installed, and so on. They were judged only on their net profit in that corporation. Each individual warehouse became almost a separate, independent, autonomous business. Through the years, really up into the fifties, this was a

highly successful thing, but by that time it had grown to something like 250 warehouses. You had something like 265 million dollars worth of sales. Everything was just put into here and went out through these branches, and they were interested in net profit. They knew what their gross profit was on_____, they knew what their gross profit was on_____, and individual studies could show what they were making on each, but as far as they were concerned their job was to buy the stuff and sell it out and make a profit and they were rewarded on that basis. They became little camps, very successful ones, developed some very strong businessmen, but two things happened. One is that markets began to separate and the ideas of where the company wanted to go and how they wanted to get there began to emerge. You had no control or no system because your whole basis of training these people and of judging them and of paying them and everything else was on them running their show in that area. We really didn't have a hold of the business, and within those businesses had emerged at least ten strongly identifiable separate kinds of business. The company did very well, *but it wasn't under control.*

Only three of the twelve corporations have moved unequivocally toward decentralization in the past decade, and one of the three is not yet fully decentralized. Five of the firms, then, have relatively stable structures, three centralized, one with a mixed pattern of decision making, and one fully decentralized. Three have moved in the direction of decentralization, while four have gone in the other direction. As a group, then, the twelve corporations have changed little over the years. Those attempting decentralization did so expecting that a system of financial controls would maintain coordination; those which have partly recentralized found that the controls alone could not do this.

Unlike finance departments, the twelve corporations employ very diverse technologies, some much more complex than others. It could be argued that technology is the main determinant of structure and decision-making patterns among these firms. Indeed, a first impression is that the centralized firms each make only a single product whereas the fully decentralized corporations manufacture a variety of items. This, I would argue, however, reflects more than anything else how managers choose to define their businesses and by implication the administrative structures which control them. One informant explained in detail how the single commodity made by his firm constrained its formal structure, but immediately added that seventeen to twenty *thousand* different products were manufactured each year. Each plant was described as a "glorified job shop." Should anyone doubt the ability of businesses to redefine their products, and hence their formal structures, I suggest he read Alfred Sloan's *My Years with General Motors.*[4]

The informal study of twelve corporations thus suggests, but by no means proves, that some of the findings from the study of finance departments may hold for all organizations. Similar relationships between formal structure, decision-making, and evaluation procedures appear among departments of finance and huge corporations, and equilibrium processes are evident in both. It is an old saw, but further research is needed, particularly longitudinal studies which would allow investigators to identify important changes and their long-term consequences in a population of organizations.

BEYOND STRUCTURAL-FUNCTIONALISM

The implications of this study for sociological theory ought to be explored briefly. The relevance of research on small bureaucratic organizations for social systems theory is by no means clear, but by the same token, the relevance of most sociological research for theory is questionable. Theory and research in sociology have gone in different directions over the years. Theory has tended to focus on large and complex groups—societies and communities—and not surprisingly it has emphasized complexity, if not uniqueness.[5] Research, on the other hand, has focused on individual people and small groups and has generated more social-psychological than sociological propositions. Furthermore, contemporary research methods in their quest for simple linear relationships among large numbers of variables tend to overlook complex relationships among small sets of variables or treat them as

[4]Alfred P. Sloan, Jr., *My Years with General Motors* (Garden City, N.Y.: Doubleday, 1964).
[5]See, for example, S. N. Eisenstadt, *Modernization: Protest and Change* (Englewood Cliffs, N.J.: Prentice-Hall, 1966). "The preceding analysis indicates that these conditions are not simply related to . . . modernization. . . . The picture is certainly much more complex. . . . The interrelationship between political and economic development has proved to be rather complicated and paradoxical . . ." (pp. 71-74).

anomalous.[6] A study of organizations such as this one attempts to bridge the gap between theory and research. On the one hand, it focuses on organizations as wholes, small social systems if you will, and considers only variables describing entire organizations, not the people in them. On the other hand, it attempts rigor, or as much rigor as seems appropriate, in using quantitative variables which are often true ratio scales, and in statistical analysis of data from a fairly large number of cases.

No single theoretical perspective dominates sociology, but the structural-functional approach has probably been more influential than any other in the past two decades. Structural-functionalism is not, to this writer, a complete theory, for it does not yield propositions that admit empirical confirmation or disconfirmation. It is rather what I would call pretheory. As far as I can tell, the structural-functionalist approach alerts the investigator to several considerations. First, it notes that although social systems are complex, they ought to be analyzed in terms of general categories—"a carefully and critically worked out system of concepts which are capable of application to all relevant parts or aspects of a concrete system in a coherent way."[7] Second, structural-functionalism focuses on consequences. It asks, according to Parsons: "What would be the differential consequences for the system of two or more alternative outcomes of a dynamic process."[8] Merton makes much the same assumption: "The central orientation of functionalism [is] expressed in the practice of interpreting data by establishing their consequences for the larger structures in which they are implicated."[9]

A number of criticisms of the structural-functionalist school have been voiced, and it is impossible to cover all of them here. One is that the approach is inherently conservative because it seeks to explain stability rather than change. Both Parsons and Merton deny this: Parsons by

[6]This is not to attack recent methodological advances; the intention is only to note that empirical methods do not yet exist for dealing with some of the most interesting sociological problems. See, for example, Hubert M. Blalock's discussion of block-recursive models in *Theory Construction* (Englewood Cliffs, N.J.: Prentice-Hall, 1969), pp. 71-74.

[7]Talcott Parsons, *The Social System* (New York: Free Press, 1951), p. 20.

[8]*Ibid.*, pp. 21-22.

[9]Robert K. Merton, "Manifest and Latent Functions," in *Social Theory and Social Structure*, 2d ed. rev. (New York: Free Press, 1957), pp. 46-47.

arguing that disorder or disorganization is always a possibility; Merton by coining the notion of dysfunctions which presumably lessen the adaptation or adjustment of social systems. Nonetheless, the debate rages on.[10] A second criticism is that the categories used by structural-functionalists are so broad, some say omnivorous, that they fail to distinguish interesting sociological phenomena from irrelevancies. Nothing, it is argued, is excluded from the purview of structural-functional analysis, hence the central task of science, the reduction of complicated data to relatively simple generalizations, is made impossible. Parsons' version of structural-functionalism does have the virtues of completeness and isomorphism. It is a global theory, and it posits similar relations among categories at different levels of analysis.[11] What it needs is Occam's razor.

A third criticism of structural-functionalism, ironically, is that it is an insufficient description of social reality. Contemporary systems theory argues that it is not enough to look at consequences of a given phenomenon; one must also look at causes, mutual interactions among variables, feedback, and purposive choice. Buckley writes:

> . . . only the modern systems approach promises to get at the full complexity of the interacting phenomena—to see not only the *causes* acting on the phenomena under study, the possible *consequences* of the phenomena, and the possible *mutual interactions* of some of these factors, but also to see the *total emergent processes* as a function of possible positive and/or negative *feedbacks,* mediated by the *selective decisions,* or "choices," of the individuals and groups directly or indirectly involved.[12]

Whether systems theory compounds the complexity of structural-functionalism or simplifies it by eliminating the notions of multiple

---

[10]The argument has subsided a bit in recent years. Its high point was Melvin Tumin's critique of Kingsley Davis and Wilbert Moore's "Some Principles of Stratification," *American Sociological Review,* 10, 1945, 242-249. See Tumin's "Critical Analysis," *American Sociological Review,* 18, 1953, 387-394, and the replies by Davis and Moore, *ibid.,* 394-398.

[11]Personality systems, social systems, and cultural systems are treated as quasi-autonomous (sometimes they are interdependent, sometimes not) and within their systems there are four basic functional imperatives—adaptation, goal-attainment, integration, and pattern-maintenance—all of which, according to Parsons, are complexly tied to one another. See, for example, Parsons' "An Outline of the Social System," in *Theories of Society,* eds. Parsons *et al.* (New York: Free Press, 1961), pp. 30-79.

[12]Walter Buckley, *Sociology and Modern Systems Theory* (Englewood Cliffs, N.J.: Prentice-Hall, 1967) p. 80.

levels of analysis and functional imperatives is unclear. Like structural-functionalism, the systems approach does not immediately yield testable propositions. It too is a pretheory, for it points to classes of phenomena that ought to be taken into account in sociological explanations, but not the phenomena themselves or their supposed interrelations.

Rather than explore further the complexities of structural-functionalism, we shall now turn to its application to research on organizations. The structural-functional approach, I think it can be shown, is best suited to case studies of organizations involving participant-observation. The participant-observer has the opportunity to gather information according to hunch or theoretical insight while his study is in progress. The range of variables he considers is not determined in advance in a fixed questionnaire. Furthermore, the participant-observer has time to take note of consequences of change in organizations, whereas survey methods do not easily discriminate between stable organizations and those on the verge of further change or readjustment. Participant-observation thus allows one to follow the directives of the structural-functional approach; survey analysis is superficial by contrast. Unfortunately, and this is not an inherent flaw of structural-functionalist theory, participant-observation has been used almost exclusively in case studies of organizations. And generalizations based on single observations are extremely tenuous and often wrong. This is why, in my opinion, structural-functionalism has not developed beyond the level of sweeping and imprecise generalizations. It remains a pretheory so long as it is tied to the case study method. The weakness of the single case method is illustrated if we compare conclusions from studies of two organizations, both conducted according to structural-functional precepts. The first is from Blau's *The Dynamics of Bureaucracy*, the second from Selznick's *TVA and the Grass Roots*.

> The only permanence in bureaucratic structure is the occurrence of change in predictable patterns, and even these are not unalterably fixed. . . . Perfect adjustment is hardly possible because the very practices instituted to enhance adjustment in some respects often disturb it in others. Hence the stable attainment of organizational objectives depends on perpetual change in the bureaucratic structure.[13]

[13]Peter M. Blau, *The Dynamics of Bureaucracy*, 2d ed. (Chicago: University of Chicago Press, 1963), p. 250.

Adaptive social structures are to be analyzed in structural-functional terms. This means that contemporary and variable behavior is related to a presumptively stable system of needs and mechanisms. Every such structure has a set of basic needs and develops systematic means of self-defense.... The needs in question are organizational, not individual, and include: the security of the organization as a whole in relation to social forces in its environment; the stability of lines of authority and communication....[14]

Blau perceives perpetual change in organizations; Selznick, by contrast, detects underlying stability protected by strategic adaptations. Though inconsistent, neither of these conclusions is inconsistent with the structural-functional framework.

How, then, do we go beyond the limitations of the case study method and at the same time preserve the focus on consequences which is central to the structural-functional perspective? Ideally, one would conduct participant-observation studies in a large number of organizations to develop generalizations. The study of finance departments fell short of this ideal, but its results point to a set of variables or of classes of variables which should be examined in comparative studies of social structures and particularly of formal organizations. Of central importance is the "authority structure," mechanisms of control and coordination which wield fairly large groups of people into working organizations. The formal hierarchy of command, procedures for evaluation, and distribution of rewards all comprise the authority structure of organizations. These variables have been dealt with extensively here. The second set of variables might be very loosely labeled "technology": how an organization divides work among its members and the tools or machinery it uses in its tasks. This too we have dealt with, to the extent that a study of government bureaucracies will permit. A third set of variables I label "organizational imperatives" which exist at both the individual and structural levels. Organizations do things for people and cease to exist, eventually, when people no longer benefit from them. One must consider what is expected of organizations by their clients and members, something we have done only implicitly by restricting the study to finance departments which do more or less the same things. Of equal importance is the imperative to maintain organization as such which may not be reducible to individual motives and interests.

[14]Philip Selznick, *TVA and the Grass Roots* (Berkeley: University of California Press, 1949), p. 252.

The most general notion to emerge from this study is that changes in technology and formal structure give rise to other structural changes intended to satisfy organizational imperatives. Both stability and change exist in organizations, but on balance, we sense that organizations are more stable than changing. More important, however, is the tentative link between change and stability we have forged. *Changes in organizations have multiple consequences, the net effect of which is no change,* at least insofar as organizational integrity or coherence are concerned. Changes in size, structure, and the degree of interdependence or self-containment bring about other changes: The supervisory ratio is decreased at some levels but increased at others; decision-making authority is decentralized but authority is centralized in the rules; the potential for interunit conflict is created, but so is the coordinator's role; the likelihood of disorganization develops, but so do mechanisms promoting feedback. At least in the short run, then, an organization's authority structure, its ability to maintain imperative coordination, remains intact. This is not to say that the situation of individual workers remains unaltered as these changes occur; quite the contrary. But it does indicate that we cannot expect the disappearance of authority, coordination, and regulation from organizations.

From the perspective of structural-functionalism, we have thus developed a hypothesis that can be confirmed or disconfirmed through further research. Authority or imperative coordination is central to organizations. Changes in organizational structure may give rise to changes in authority patterns, but other modifications occur which tend to restore coordination. Any single change is thus hypothesized to have complex and contradictory effects, at least in the short run. Changes over longer time intervals are less predictable; they no doubt reflect environmental conditions which for the most part cannot be controlled by organizations.

INDIVIDUAL RATIONALITY
IN ORGANIZATIONAL SETTINGS

We should now return to the questions raised at the beginning of this study: Is the rationality of bureaucratic organizations inimical to what is rational for individual persons as Mannheim foresaw? Does bureaucratization inevitably lead to centralization of control in society and the loss of people's capacity to use their "insights into the interrelations of events"? These questions do not admit simple answers, nor will techniques of empirical research alone generate all the information needed to arrive at even tentative conclusions. About the best we can do is develop some understanding of the direction in which administrative structures are changing, if they are changing at all, and ask how this affects the prospects for individual rationality in organizational settings. To observe long-term changes in patterns of organization does not contradict the earlier claim that equilibrium or persistence characterizes most administrative structures. What persists or remains in equilibrium is an organization's ability to elicit more or less predictable behavior from its members, to maintain imperative coordination. Changes in structure or operating procedures may occur, but they stimulate other changes which have the effect of maintaining organizational integrity or coherence.

Weber's model of bureaucracy is now widely discarded as obsolete, as an incomplete and inconsistent description of organizations. Before laying it to rest, several observations about the ideal-typical model are required. First, Weber was discussing a form of administration that was relatively new and historically unique at the time he was writing. It was technically rational insofar as it formalized rules, responsibilities, and the systematic filing of records. It was rational for individual bureaucrats because they had the assurance of a career, social esteem, and other emoluments of office. And it was rational for advanced societies insofar as it assured fair and impartial application of laws and administrative codes. To be sure, what Weber praised about bureaucracy others have damned. Particularly controversial is Weber's notion that democracy is best promoted by the "leveling" of the masses in the face of the omnipotent bureaucratic apparatus of the state.[15] Mannheim's doubts about the rationality of large-scale organizations stem directly from this supposed virtue of bureaucracy.

Let me apply a label to Weberian bureaucracy and call it "simple centralized administration." It is simple because bureaucrats need but obey the imperative to act according to the rules. Its formal structure is also simple and strictly hierarchical: Nonvertical ties are not allowed.

---

[15]Max Weber, "Bureaucracy," in *From Max Weber: Essays in Sociology*, eds. H. Gerth and C. W. Mills (New York: Oxford University Press, 1958), pp. 224-228.

Weber's model of bureaucracy is also centralized because cases to which rules and codes do not apply are automatically referred to higher levels; discretion simply does not exist for bureaucrats who deal directly with clients. Functional rationality, to use Mannheim's language, pervades this structure; one behaves according to criteria set for him by others. Although possibly obsolete, simple centralized administration is still widely used. Some of the smaller departments of finance still fit this pattern if our inferences are correct. Crozier's account of French administration in *The Bureaucratic Phenomenon* portrays vividly the dysfunctions, and tenaciousness, of the simple centralized form or organization.[16]

The limits of the simple centralized form of administration are not known. At one extreme, the Orwellian vision of 1984 imagines a society which is centrally controlled and tolerant of no deviation whatsoever. At the other, some commentators predict a transformation of beliefs which would render formal administrative structures unnecessary to secure cooperative effort.[17] Neither of these outcomes is likely if our data on finance departments in any way anticipate what is taking place in organizations. Stability is paramount, but at the same time incremental changes are occurring in the direction of greater complexity and decentralization of authority. Complexity intrudes into organizations once it is admitted that objectives cannot be wholly determined in advance by one or two top managers. The hierarchical structure becomes something other than a chain of command as workers on different levels are drawn into the process of transforming nonoperational goals into operational programs of behavior. Complexity further intrudes when horizontal lines of communication are superimposed on otherwise neat vertical tables of organization. Decentralization emerges as rules, and regulations specify criteria to be used in making decisions, but not decisions themselves. And it spreads as work is reorganized into self-contained units which are potentially autonomous of the larger organization.

The movement away from simple centralized administration, to the extent that it is occurring, does not so much reflect the demand for efficiency as the trend toward incorporating other values into organiza-

[16]Michel Crozier, *The Bureaucratic Phenomenon* (Chicago: University of Chicago Press, 1964).
[17]See, for example, Charles A. Reich, *The Greening of America* (New York: Random House, 1970).

tions. There is the increasing insistence that organizations act responsibly in dealing with their members, clients, and the public.[18] In addition, attitudes toward authority are changing rapidly. Rules and commands which once would have been uncritically accepted now require justification. This is ironic, for it is primarily the bureaucratic agencies of government which make new demands and place new restrictions on private organizations, and bureaucratically organized school systems which teach people the values of autonomy and self-realization. All this is not to say that simple centralized administration necessarily carries the seeds of its own destruction. But it is transformed inextricably once human and esthetic values are made as salient as economic ones. Add to this the strain toward equality and resistance to governmental authority in U.S. society,[19] and the likelihood of a centralized and totally bureaucratized state seems slight indeed.

A central theme in sociological studies of organizations is the strain between organizational imperatives and the needs and intentions of members and clients. Here we have been concerned with the assertion that coordination and control in organizations is inimical to what is rational for individual persons insofar as it substitutes organizational (or functional) rationality for individual (or substantial) rationality. The research suggests that coordination and control rarely disappear from organizations but do take different forms, some clearly antithetical to individual autonomy, others supportive of it. Control by direct command has very different implications for rationality than the maintenance of order through established standards of performance, which is in turn different from the use of consensual mechanisms. Because such variations exist among organizations, the research also suggests that sweeping statements about the nature of bureaucracy or large-scale organizations in general are apt to be misleading. To assert that organizations undermine rationality is to overlook the ways in which they protect rationality.

One remaining question concerns variables not taken into account here, particularly those describing the legal, social, and cultural contents in which administrative agencies operate. Organizational forms are to

---

[18]See George F. F. Lombard, "Relativism in Organizations," *Harvard Business Review*, 49, no. 2, March-April, 1971, 55-65.
[19]Value orientations in U.S. society are discussed by S. M. Lipset in *The First New Nation* (New York: Basic Books, 1963).

some extent derivative from their settings. The idea of a formal hierarchy of command, for example, has very different meanings depending on whether the overt exercise of authority is welcomed or rejected in a society. How different meanings are translated into practice is a moot question which will only be answered by research that considers large numbers of organizations in different societies. A tentative hypothesis is that the continuum from simple centralized to complex and decentralized administration accounts for most differences in organizational patterns regardless of societal characteristics. A common pattern of change of organizational forms away from Weberian-type bureaucracy is thus posited.

The chances for substantial rationality, the "capacity to act intelligently in a given situation on the basis of one's own insights into the interrelations of events," are most likely enhanced by the trend away from simple centralized administrative structures. Intelligent action presupposes choices, and choices become available only where competing and even disparate values are present. Bureaucracy, as Weber described it, embodies the value of efficiency but rejects other bases for action. New forms of organization, organizations which are constrained to maximize efficiency and other values as well, do not suffer this limitation. Organizational rationality becomes a matter of reconciling sets of values rather than maximizing one, and this process demands much of human rationality.

Bibliography*

Aiken, Michael, and Jerald Hage, "Organizational alienation: A comparative analysis," *American Sociological Review* 31 (1966) 497-507.

Aiken, Michael, and Jerald Hage, "Organizational interdependence and intraorganizational structure," *American Sociological Review* 33 (1968): 912-930.

Akers, Ronald L., and Richard Quinney, "Differential organization of health professions: A comparative analysis," *American Sociological Review* 33 (1968): 104-121.

Anderson, Theodore R., and Seymour Warkov, "Organizational size and functional complexity: A study of administration in hospitals," *American Sociological Review* 26 (1961): 23-28.

Armstrong, John A., "Sources of administrative behavior: Some Soviet and Western European comparisons," *American Political Science Review* 59 (1965): 643-655.

Baum, Bernard H., Peter F. Sorensen, Jr., and William S. Place, "Patterns of consensus in the perception of organizational control," *Sociological Quarterly* 10 (1969): 335-340.

Becker, Selwyn W., and Nicholas Baloff, "Organization structure and complex problem solving," *Administrative Science Quarterly* 14 (1969): 260-271.

Becker, Selwyn W., and Gerald Gordon, "An entrepreneurial theory of formal organizations. Part I. Patterns of formal organizations," *Administrative Science Quarterly* 11 (1966): 315-344.

Bendix, Reinhard, "Industrialization, ideologies, and social structure," *American Sociological Review* 24 (1959): 613-623.

Bendix, Reinhard, "Concepts and generalizations in comparative sociological studies," *American Sociological Review* 28 (1963): 532-539.

Bennis, Warren, "Beyond bureaucracy," *Trans-Action* 2 (1965): 31-35.

Berger, Morroe, "Bureaucracy East and West," *Administrative Science Quarterly* 1 (1957): 518-529.

*The bibliography includes *articles* in which structural features of organizations were considered.

Berk, Bernard B., "Organizational goals and inmate organization," *American Journal of Sociology* 71 (1966): 522-534.

Blankenship, L. Vaughn, and Raymond E. Miles, "Organizational structure and managerial decision behavior," *Administrative Science Quarterly* 13 (1968): 106-120.

Blau, Peter M., "Social integration, social rank, and processes of interaction," *Human Organization* 18 (1959-60): 152-157.

Blau, Peter M., "Comparative study of organizations," *Industrial and Labor Relations Review* 18 (1965): 323-338.

Blau, Peter M., "The hierarchy of authority in organizations," *American Journal of Sociology* 73 (1968): 453-467.

Blau, Peter M., "A formal theory of differentiation in organizations," *American Sociological Review* 35 (1970): 201-218.

Blau, Peter M., Wolf v. Heydebrand, and Robert Stauffer, "The structure of small bureaucracies," *American Sociological Review* 31 (1966): 179-191.

Bowers, David G., "Organizational control in an insurance company," *Sociometry,* 27 (1964): 230-244.

Brewer, John, "Flow of communications, expert qualifications and organizational authority structures," *American Sociological Review* 36 (1971): 475-484.

Burack, Elmer H., "Industrial management in advanced production systems: Some theoretical concepts and preliminary findings," *Administrative Science Quarterly* 12 (1967): 479-500.

Carzo, Rocco, Jr., and John N. Yanouzas, "Effects of flat and tall organization structure," *Administrative Science Quarterly* 14 (1969): 178-191.

Chapin, F. Stuart, "The growth of bureaucracy: An hypothesis," *American Sociological Review* 16 (1951): 835-856.

Chapin, F. Stuart, and John E. Tsouderos, "Formalization observed in ten voluntary associations: Concepts, morphology, process," *Social Forces* 33 (1955): 306-309.

Childers, Grant W., Bruce H. Mayhew, Jr., and Louis N. Gray, "System size and structural differentiation in military organizations: Testing a baseline model of the division of labor," *American Journal of Sociology* 76 (1971): 813-830.

Clark, Burton R., "Organizational adaptation and precarious values," *American Sociological Review* 21 (1956): 327-336.

Coser, Rose Laub, "Authority and decision-making in a hospital: A comparative analysis," *American Sociological Review* 23 (1958): 56-63.

Crane, Diana, "Scientists at major and minor universities: A study of productivity and recognition," *American Sociological Review* 30 (1965): 699-714.

Cressey, Donald R., "Contradictory directives in complex organizations: The case of the prison," *Administrative Science Quarterly* 4 (1959): 1-19.

Crozier, Michel, "The present convergence of public administration and large private enterprises, and its consequences," *International Social Science Journal* 20 (1968): 7-16.

Dill, William R., "Environment as an influence on managerial autonomy," *Administrative Science Quarterly* 2 (1958): 409-443.

Draper, Jean, and George B. Strother, "Testing a model for organizational growth," *Human Organization* 22 (1963): 180-194.

Dutton, John M., and Richard E. Walton, "Interdepartmental conflict and cooperation: Two contrasting studies," *Human Organization* 25 (1966): 207-220.

Eisenstadt, S. N., "Some reflections on the variability of development and organizational structures," *Administrative Science Quarterly* 13 (1968): 491-497.

Elling, Ray H., and Sandor Halebsky, "Organizational differentiation and support: A conceptual framework," *Administrative Science Quarterly* 6 (1961): 185-209.

Entwisle, Doris R., and John Walton, "Observations on the span of control," *Administrative Science Quarterly* 5 (1961): 522-533.

Faunce, William A., "Size of locals and union democracy," *American Journal of Sociology* 68 (1962): 291-298.

Fouraker, Lawrence E., and John M. Stopford, "Organizational structure and multinational strategy," *Administrative Science Quarterly* 13 (1968): 47-64.

Georgopoulos, Basil H., and Arnold S. Tannenbaum, "A study of organizational effectiveness," *American Sociological Review* 22 (1957): 534-540.

Goldthorpe, John H., Technical organization as a factor in supervisor-worker conflict," *British Journal of Sociology* 10 (1959): 213-230.

Grusky, Oscar, "Corporate size, bureaucratization, and managerial succession," *American Journal of Sociology* 67 (1961): 261-269.

Guest, Robert H., "Managerial succession in complex organizations," *American Journal of Sociology* 68 (1962): 47-56.

Haas, J. Eugene, and Linda Collen, "Administrative practices in university departments," *Administrative Science Quarterly* 8 (1963): 44-60.

Haas, J. Eugene, Richard H. Hall, and Norman J. Johnson, "The size of the supportive component in organizations: A multi-organizational analysis," *Social Forces* 42 (1963): 9-17.

Hage, Jerald, "An axiomatic theory of organizations," *Administrative Science Quarterly* 10 (1965): 289-320.

Hage, Jerald, and Michael Aiken, "Program change and organizational properties: A comparative analysis," *American Journal of Sociology* 72 (1967): 503-519.

Hage, Jerald, and Michael Aiken, "Relationship of centralization to other organizational properties," *Administrative Science Quarterly* 12 (1967): 72-92.

Hage, Jerald, and Michael Aiken, "Routine technology, social structure and organizational goals," *Administrative Science Quarterly* 14 (1969): 366-376.

Hage, Jerald, Michael Aiken, and Cora Bagley Marrett, "Organization structure and communications," *American Sociological Review* 36 (1971): 860-871.

Haire, Mason, "Biological models and empirical histories of the growth of organizations," pp. 272-306 in Mason Haire (ed.), *Modern Organization Theory* (New York: Wiley, 1959).

Haire, Mason, Edwin E. Ghiselli, and Lyman W. Porter, "Cultural patterns in the role of the manager," *Industrial Relations* 2 (1963): 95-117.

Hall, Richard H., "Intraorganizational structural variation: Application of the bureaucratic model," *Administrative Science Quarterly* 7 (1962): 295-308.

Hall, Richard H., "Bureaucracy and small organizations," *Sociology and Social Research* 48 (1963): 38-46.

Hall, Richard H., "The concept of bureaucracy: An empirical assessment," *American Journal of Sociology* 69 (1963): 32-40.

Hall, Richard H., "Some organizational considerations in the professional-organizational relationship," *Administrative Science Quarterly* 12 (1967): 461-478.

Hall, Richard H., "Professionalization and bureaucratization," *American Sociological Review* 33 (1968): 92-104.

Hall, Richard H., J. Eugene Haas, and Norman J. Johnson, "Organizational size, complexity, and formalization," *American Sociological Review* 32 (1967): 903-912.

Hall, Richard H., J. Eugene Haas, and Norman J. Johnson, "An examination of the Blau-Scott and Etzioni typologies," *Administrative Science Quarterly* 12 (1967): 118-139.

Hall, Richard H., and Charles R. Tittle, "A note on bureaucracy and its correlates," *American Journal of Sociology* 72 (1966): 267-272.

Hebden, J. E., M. J. Rose, and W. H. Scott, "Management structure and computerization," *Sociology* 3 (1969): 377-396.

Heller, Frank A., "Studies in organisations: The effect of structure on industrial relations," *Journal of Industrial Relations* 2 (1960): 1-19.

Hickson, David J., D. S. Pugh, and Diana C. Pheysey, "Operations technology and organization structure: An empirical reappraisal," *Administrative Science Quarterly* 14 (1969): 378-397.

Hinings, C. R., D. S. Pugh, D. J. Hickson, and C. Turner, "An approach to the study of bureaucracy," *Sociology* 1 (1967): 61-72.

Holdaway, Edward A., and Thomas A. Blowers, "Administrative ratios and organization size: a longitudinal examination," *American Sociological Review* 36 (1971): 278-286.

Hummon, Norman P., "A mathematical theory of differentiation in organizations," *American Sociological Review* 36 (1971): 297-303.

Indik, Bernard P., "The relationship between organization size and supervision ratio," *Administrative Science Q uarterly* 9 (1964): 301-312.

Indik, Bernard P., "Organization size and member participation: Some empirical tests of alternative explanations," *Human Relations* 18 (1965): 339-350.

Ingham, Geoffrey K., Organizational size, orientation to work and industrial behavior," *Sociology* 1 (1967): 239-258.

Inkson, J. H. K., D. S. Pugh, and D. J. Hickson, "Organization context and structure: An abbreviated replication," *Administrative Science Quarterly* 15 (1970): 318-329.

Julian, Joseph, "Compliance patterns and communication blocks in complex organizations," *American Sociological Review* 31 (1966): 382-389.

Kaufman, Herbert, and David Seidman, "The morphology of organizations," *Administrative Science Quarterly* 15 (1970): 439-451.

Klatzky, S. R., "Organizational inequality: The case of the public employment agencies," *American Journal of Sociology* 76 (1970): 474-491.

Klatzky, S. R., "Relationship of organizational size to complexity and coordination," *Administrative Science Quarterly* 15 (1970): 428-438.

Kriesberg, Louis, "Careers, organization size, and succession," *American Journal of Sociology* 68 (1962): 355-359.

Kunz, Phillip R., "Sponsorship and organizational stability: Boy Scout Troops," *American Journal of Sociology* 74 (1969): 666-675.

Landsberger, Henry A., "The horizontal dimension in bureaucracy," *Administrative Science Quarterly* 6 (1961): 299-332.

Lawrence, Paul R., and Jay W. Lorsch, "Differentiation and integration in complex organizations," *Administrative Science Quarterly* 12 (1967): 1-48.

Levinson, Daniel J., "Role, personality, and social structure in the organizational setting," *Journal of Abnormal and Social Psychology* 58 (1959): 170-180.

Lieberson, Stanley, "An empirical study of military-industrial linkages," *American Journal of Sociology* 76 (1971): 562-584.

Litwak, Eugene, "Models of organizations which permit conflict," *American Journal of Sociology* 67 (1961): 177-184.

Litwak, Eugene, and Lydia F. Hylton, "Interorganizational analysis: A hypothesis on co-ordinating agencies," *Administrative Science Quarterly* 6 (1962): 395-420.

McNulty, James E., "Organizational change in growing enterprises," *Administrative Science Quarterly* 7 (1962): 1-20.

McWhinney, W. H., "On the geometry of organizations," *Administrative Science Quarterly,* 10 (1965): 347-363.

Martin, Roderick, "Union democracy: An explanatory framework," *Sociology* 2 (1968): 205-220.

Meltzer, Leo, and James Salter, "Organizational structure and the performance and job satisfaction of physiologists," *American Sociological Review* 27 (1962): 351-362.

Meyer, John W., "High school effects on college intentions," *American Journal of Sociology* 76 (1970): 59-70.

Meyer, Marshall W., "Two authority structures of bureaucratic organization," *Administrative Science Quarterly* 13 (1968): 211-228.

Meyer, Marshall W., "Automation and bureaucratic structure," *American Journal of Sociology* 74 (1968): 256-264.

Meyer, Marshall W., "Expertness and the span of control," *American Sociological Review* 33 (1968): 944-951.

Meyer, Marshall W., "Some constraints in analyzing data on organizational structures," *American Sociological Review* 36 (1971): 294-297.

Peabody, Robert L., "Perceptions of organizational authority: A comparative analysis," *Administrative Science Quarterly* 6 (1962): 463-482.

Perrow, Charles, "The analysis of goals in complex organizations," *American Sociological Review* 26 (1961): 854-865.

Perrow, Charles, "A framework for the comparative analysis of organizations," *American Sociological Review* 32 (1967): 194-208.

Perrucci, Robert, and Mark Pilisuk, "Leaders and ruling elites: The interorganizational bases of community power," *American Sociological Review* 35 (1970): 1040-1056.

Pondy, Louis R., "Effects of size, complexity, and ownership on administrative intensity," *Administrative Science Quarterly* 14 (1969): 47-60.

Presthus, Robert V., "Weberian v. welfare bureaucracy in traditional society," *Administrative Science Quarterly* 6 (1961): 1-24.

Pugh, D. S., D. J. Hickson, and C. R. Hinings, "An empirical taxonomy of structures of work organizations," *Administrative Science Quarterly* 14 (1969): 115-126.

Pugh, D. S., D. J. Hickson, C. R. Hinings, and C. Turner, "Dimensions of organizational structure," *Administrative Science Quarterly* 13 (1968): 65-105.

Pugh, D. S., D. J. Hickson, C. R. Hinings, and C. Turner, "The context of organization structures," *Administrative Science Quarterly* 14 (1969): 91-114.

Pugh, D. S., D. J. Hickson, C. R. Hinings, K. M. MacDonald, C. Turner, and T. Lupton, "A conceptual scheme for organizational analysis," *Administrative Science Quarterly* 8 (1963): 301-307.

Raphael, Edna E., "Power structure and membership dispersion in unions," *American Journal of Sociology* 71 (1965): 274-283.

Raphael, Edna E., "The Anderson-Warkov hypothesis in local unions: A comparative study," *American Sociological Review* 32 (1967): 768-776.

Richardson, Stephen A., "Organizational contrasts on British and American ships," *Administrative Science Quarterly* 1 (1956): 189-207.

Rose, Arnold M., "Voluntary associations under conditions of competition and conflict," *Social Forces* 34 (1955): 159-163.

Rosengren, William R., "Institutional types and sociological research: An hypothesis in role systems and research models," *Human Organization* 20 (1961): 42-48.

Rosengren, William, R., "Communication, organization, and conduct in the therapeutic milieu," *Administrative Science Quarterly* 9 (1964): 70-90.

Rosengren, William R., "Structure, policy, and style: Strategies of organizational control," *Administrative Science Quarterly* 12 (1967): 140-164.

Rosengren, William R., and Mark Lefton, "Organizations and clients: Lateral and longitudinal dimensions," *American Sociological Review* 31 (1966): 802-810.

Rosner, Martin M., "Economic determinants of organizational innovation," *Administrative Science Quarterly* 12 (1968): 614-625.

Rushing, William A., "Organizational size and administration: The problems of causal homogeneity and a heterogeneous category," *Pacific Sociological Review* 9 (1966): 100-108.

Rushing, William A., "The effects of industry size and division of labor on administration," *Administrative Science Quarterly* 12 (1967): 273-295.

Rushing, William A., "Hardness of material as related to division of labor in manufacturing industries," *Administrative Science Quarterly* 13 (1968): 229-245.

Samuel, Yitzhak, and Bilha F. Mannheim, "A multidimensional approach toward a typology of bureaucracy," *Administrative Science Quarterly* 15 (1970): 216-228.

Scott, Joseph W., and Mohamed El-Assal, "Multiversity, university size, university quality, and student protest: An empirical study," *American Sociological Review* 34 (1969): 702-722.

Scott, W. Richard, Sanford M. Dornbusch, Bruce C. Busching, and James D. Laing, "Organizational evaluation and authority," *Administrative Science Quarterly* 12 (1967): 93-117.

Seashore, Stanley E., and Ephraim Yuchtman, "Factorial analysis of organizational performance," *Administrative Science Quarterly* 12 (1967): 377-395.

Simon, Abraham J., "Social structure of clinics and patient improvement," *Administrative Science Quarterly* 4 (1959): 197-206.

Simpson, Richard L., and William H. Gulley, "Goals, environmental pressures, and organizational characteristics," *American Sociological Review* 27 (1962): 344-351.

Smith, Clagett G., "A comparative analysis of some conditions and consequences of intra-organizational conflict," *Administrative Science Quarterly* 10 (1966): 504-529.

Smith, Clagett G., and Oguz Ari, "Organizational control structure and member consensus," *American Journal of Sociology* 69 (1964): 623-638.

Smith, Clagett G., and Arnold S. Tannenbaum, "Organizational control structure: A comparative analysis," *Human Relations* 16 (1963): 299-316.

Sofer, Cyril, "Reactions to administrative change," *Human Relations* 8 (1955): 291-316.

Starbuck, William H., "Organizational growth and development," in James G. March (ed.), *Handbook of Organizations* (Chicago: Rand McNally, 1965).

Stinchcombe, Arthur L., "Bureaucratic and craft administration of production: A comparative study," *Administrative Science Quarterly* 4 (1959): 168-187.

Tannenbaum, Arnold S., "Control structure and union functions," *American Journal of Sociology* 61 (1956): 536-545.

Tannenbaum, Arnold S., "Control and effectiveness in a voluntary organization," *American Journal of Sociology* 67 (1961): 33-46.

Tannenbaum, Arnold S., and Basil S. Georgopoulos, "The distribution of control in formal organizations," *Social Forces* 36 (1957): 44-50.

Terrien, Frederic W., and Donald L. Mills, "The effect of changing size upon the internal structure of organizations," *American Sociological Review* 20 (1955): 11-13.

Thomas, Edwin J., "Role conceptions and organizational size," *American Sociological Review* 24 (1959): 30-37.

Thompson, James D., "Authority and power in 'identical' organizations," *American Journal of Sociology* 62 (1956): 290-301.

Thompson, James D., "Organizational management of conflict," *Administrative Science Quarterly* 4 (1960): 389-409.

Thompson, James D., and Frederick L. Bates, "Technology, organization, and administration," *Administrative Science Quarterly* 2 (1957): 325-343.

Thompson, James D., and William J. McEwen, "Organizational goals and environment: Goal setting as an interaction process," *American Sociological Review* 23 (1958): 23-31.

Thompson, Victor A., "Bureaucracy and innovation," *Administrative Science Quarterly* 10 (1965): 1-20.

Tsouderos, John E., "Organizational change in terms of a series of selected variables," *American Sociological Review* 20 (1955): 206-210.

Turk, Herman, "Interorganizational networks in urban society: Initial perspectives and comparative research," *American Sociological Review* 35 (1970): 1-18.

Udell, Jon G., "An empirical test of hypotheses related to span of control," *Administrative Science Quarterly* 12 (1967): 420-439.

Udy, Stanley, Jr., "Bureaucratic elements in organizations: Some research findings," *American Sociological Review* 23 (1958): 415-417.

Udy, Stanley, Jr., "Bureaucracy and rationality in Weber's organization theory: An empirical study, *American Sociological Review* 24 (1959): 791-795.

Warner, W. Keith, and A. Eugene Havens, "Goal displacement and the intangibility of organizational goals," *Administrative Science Quarterly* 12 (1968): 539-555.

Warner, W. Keith, and James S. Hilander, "The relationship between size of organization and membership participation," *Rural Sociology* 29 (1964): 30-39.

Warner, W. Keith, and Sidney J. Miller, "Organizational problems in two types of voluntary associations," *American Journal of Sociology* 69 (1964): 654-657.

Warren, Roland L., "The interorganizational field as a focus for investigation," *Administrative Science Quarterly* 12 (1967): 396-419.

Warriner, Charles K., and Jane Emery Prather, "Four types of voluntary associations," *Sociological Inquiry* 35 (1965): 138-148.

Yuchtman, Ephraim, and Stanley Seashore, "A system resource approach to organizational effectiveness," *American Sociological Review* 32 (1967): 891-903.

Zaid, Mayer N., "Power balance and staff conflict in correctional institutions,' *Administrative Science Quarterly* 7 (1962): 22-49.

Index

72 73 74 7 6 5 4 3 2 1